# A LIFE WELL LIVED
## C. Kenneth Eppert

Copyright © 2021 by C. Kenneth Eppert. All rights reserved.

The views and opinions expressed in this work are those of the author and do not necessarily reflect the views and opinions of Braughler Books LLC.

This book or any portion thereof may not be reproduced or used in any manner whatsoever without the express written permission of the publisher except for the use of brief quotations in a scholarly work or book review. For permissions or further information contact Braughler Books LLC at:

info@braughlerbooks.com

Cover and title page photo of Purple Heart: Jim Barber/Shutterstock.com

Printed in the United States of America
Published by Braughler Books LLC., Springboro, Ohio

First printing, 2021

ISBN: 978-1-955791-13-7
Library of Congress Control Number: 2021920489

Ordering information: Special discounts are available on quantity purchases by bookstores, corporations, associations, and others. For details, contact the publisher at:

sales@braughlerbooks.com
or at 937-58-BOOKS

For questions or comments about this book, please write to:

info@braughlerbooks.com

Pietro, Steve, Scott, Pops, Todd and Doug

# FOREWORD
## Thoughts from Your Sons

## Editor's Note:

I just wanted to say that being able to edit my grandfather's book was such an honor and privilege. I am so grateful that he wrote this book for not only himself, but for his entire family. He was one of the most selfless and proud people I have ever known, and I am thankful to do something for him, as he has done everything for his family. Thank you, Grandpa, I love and miss you so much.

*Andrea Shirley Eppert*

Dad,

What means the most to me, is your consideration of my input and feelings, on you getting remarried. Here I am, a very young teenager, having an adult discussion on something that would affect the entire Eppert family, from that point on. Then, I'm your best man for your wedding to Marilyn. The importance of these two events will stay with me forever. So, tonight, while you're enjoying your birthday with family and friends, remember how truly important these two events were in the life of our family. You know I would be there, if your birthday was not in November. Linda and I are doing our best to follow the warm weather. Lows in the fifties, highs between seventy and eighty degrees. I will be with you in spirit and will see you in the spring.

Love,

*Steve and Linda*

## Our Hero

You are a tough, old Marine with a heart of gold. Your legacy is your family, you fought for our freedom and then showed us how to use it. You have brought four sons into this world who are completely different. I think I can speak for all of us, when I say we have felt your love and support all of our lives.

A wise man once told me, that you are lucky to have one good dog in your lifetime. Pops, you had two good women in your lifetime, and that sure says a lot about you.

You received a special, well-deserved honor, when you took part in the "Tri-State Honor Flight." Your day in the sun, and you were worried about my feelings, because you did not ask me to chaperone you. My brother, Scott, got the honor. I just want you to know, that the love you and Marilyn instilled in us, far surpasses any jealousy that my brothers and I could ever have for each other. We are just glad you got your day, not everybody does. The best part of your trip for me, was when you arrived back at the airport to your hero's welcome home. I gave you a hug and you proclaimed, "This is as good as Washington!" Of course, that would be your reaction, because you were surrounded by friends and family, just the way you like it.

You are a man of character and integrity and I AM HONORED TO BE YOUR SON! From your sons, your grandchildren, and everybody else you have touched in your 86 years. Let me just say, YOU ARE, AND ALWAYS WILL BE OUR HERO!

All my love

*Doug*

# What is a Man?

In today's broken world, the measure of who a man is supposed to be gets very clouded. I am reminded every day in my work life and observing what goes on in the media, that priorities are very much out of line with who a man should be. Isn't it strange, that even though there is no written rule for what a truly good man is, I somehow feel very confident that I know?

I see men chasing fame, fortune, and I see them constantly looking to take the easy path or to step over others to get where they want to go. Sometimes, this is a challenge for me. When someone who works for me messes up, do I follow the negative culture and attack the person, or attack the problem? Sometimes, the easy path is to cast blame on them, and take the heat off of me, but I have learned to build, not break people, because you taught me that it isn't the measure of a man to destroy. It is more important to build, and to love — even in our work relationships. I have been told by my sales team that "I have integrity;" that "I have their back;" and, "I am the best boss they ever had." This is because of what I was taught.

I also see men around me taking shortcuts. For them, you can simply not care, and do less than what you should, and just get by, but that's not really a manly solution either. The toughest times, are when you have to take the minority position, stand up, and do the right thing. But, who determines what is right? God ... our inner dialogue ... or example? Maybe all three, but the most apparent reasons for me, come from my heavenly and earthly father.

Should I buy a better house, or save for college? Should I care that my boss or even some of my coworkers have better cars or houses than mine, when I know I work harder than they do, and shoulder more of the stress? Should I complain when they take credit for my work, and then earn more money than I do from it?

The answer to these questions is obviously NO. I have learned that living with more does not mean you live better. The pillars of a man are his family, his wife, his parents, and his friends. Without those, his house is one built of straw.

Character is something that is earned. For a man, by example, it is learned from our fathers, our brothers, our uncles, and our friends. We all have to choose the path we want to go on, and we all have to essentially choose what kind of man we want to be.

My father chose a path that was centered on simple things. He chose a path of honor. He has honored his country. He honored  two wonderful women as wives. He has honored his children by loving them, respecting them, nurturing them, teaching them what is right and wrong, and providing for them. He has honored his grandkids and great grandkids — always present, and always taking an interest in each of them personally. He honored his employer by always working hard, and going above the easy way. He honors his friends. He honors strangers, with the golden rule, rising above the times to see the good in all people, no matter what color, race, or religion.

He honors needier people than him by giving, which he still does, even at 86. He has honored God every day.

I count myself lucky that I have been given the gift to be my father's son. To be the son of a Godly man. A man who puts more value in his Lord, his country, his family, than he does in things. A man who taught my brothers to be good men, like him, to further cast his die in me and give me other examples of who I might strive to be. A man who taught me how to choose the right friends.

A man who taught me how to sacrifice for others, and not put myself first. A man who taught me how to love, how to be humble, how to NOT mistake pride in material things, but to only spend that capital when it comes to being proud of a hard day's work, or a child's accomplishment, or the loving beauty of your wife. A man who forgives, rather than holding onto anger. A man who is simple — not overcomplicated with priorities. A man, who taught me the most valuable lesson a man can learn, how to be a father.

We all have many teachers.

I may not be the best at being me yet, but with God's help and your example, Dad, I hope someday my kids, my wife, my friends, and my family will say just one tenth of the things about me, that I hold in my heart for you. More importantly, I hope that the legacy you leave will be something I can help carry on for your family (and not just in the men), and we can continue to teach many future generations of Eppert men what it means to be someone's "Pops."

It really is amazing to me, whenever people see you, or talk to you, or bring you up — even when you are not around — they always have a smile on their faces. We worry about so much in life — things we cannot control. The one thing we can control, is when we smile. To be the kind of man who makes people stop what they're doing, if only to smile because of you, is power that I think comes from being a good man. I am proud of you for learning, so effortlessly, how to have that special superhero power.

I love you, and you are a part of me pops, now and forever!

*Scott*

## Principles I Learned from My Dad

When I think about who I am, I certainly can look back at many influences in my life. My family, my relationship with Jesus, friends, work, church, sports teams, schools, and a host of other things have led to who I am today. However, when I think about the most influential things in life, it is difficult to not start with my Dad. I remember him "welcoming" me into manhood by allowing me to work with him on the camper and the furnace, and putting a new roof on our house, but that is not what imprinted on my life. What meant the most to me, were the principles he lived by and those shaped me and are now evident in my life.

First and foremost, Dad taught me the meaning of integrity and character. Two attributes I see as fundamental in all areas of life. Approaching life with character and integrity has always helped me to be successful and has allowed me to become a leader of many people. People want to follow someone that they trust, and they can't trust you if you don't have integrity and a strong character. I owe a lot of my success to these two key, core principles.

Dad always prioritized family. I have no idea how hard it must have been for him, Steve, and Doug when they lost Shirley, but I have heard enough stories that it is clear that Dad was tough. More importantly, he wanted them to stick together, and I have one of those examples in my basement now, which is the pool table we all grew up shooting on, with friends and family. What I know, and did personally witness, was how he always made time for me and my activities. Whether it was baseball or soccer, Boy Scouts, or drums in the band, Dad was always there for me. To this day, Dad is still at every event he can make for my boys and my brothers' children. Family is important, bottom line, and you make time for them, no matter what. I hope my boys will say the same thing about me someday, and set this as a guiding principle in their own lives.

I would say the next thing imprinted in my life was hard work. Do your best, no matter what, and work as hard as you can to get the job

done! One of my best examples of Dad working hard was when he had to go to off-shift to work. Somehow, Dad still found time to support my sports and music, even though he was tired and working to support our family. When I got older, I felt the pressure early in my career, whether he knows it or not, when Dad invited me into the company he worked for, Ilsco. He approached the VP of Ops at the time, Dave Flynn, and asked if he needed help. That conversation launched my career in operations, where it was expected that you work hard, serve customers, and do it right the first time. Many nights at the dinner table, Dad and I would talk about work and he would "coach" me on how to approach things. I will always remember those dinner conversations and the council on working hard, listening to others, and valuing everyone on the team.

The last core principle was humility and understanding that I am not the center of the universe. Dad is a humble man…he is proud of his family and his service, but it is not an arrogance. Every time we get together as a family at a holiday, Dad tells us how proud he is of his family, and there is never a dry eye when he gets done. This side of him came out later in life, but it has been hugely impactful. This principle is also what showed us the importance of God and a relationship with Jesus. We always went to church, but it was in my 20s when Dad and I attended a Promise Keepers convention together. One day, during the altar call, we both went up… when we got there, we both said that we felt the pull of the Holy Spirit to come and get prayer, and we both hoped the other would come up as well. It is interesting how a consistent attitude of reverence and humility imprints on your life. I know I can trust that my heavenly Father loves me because I see how much my earthly Father loves me!

Thank you, Dad, for imprinting on my life these core principles in my life. I am who I am today, because of your investment in my life.

*Todd*

It was Easter 2007 when we first met. My wife, my daughter and I had been in the US only for few days. Far from home, we were trying to understand the lay of the land, with mixed feelings that were difficult to explain, something between excitement and confusion. Being invited to join your family for Easter was a great surprise, unexpected and somehow intimidating. Will our limited ability to communicate be a problem? Will we be capable of fitting in with the company, or will we be spending the majority of the party talking to each other in a corner? Well, that night on our way back home, I could not stop thinking about this strange sensation: for the first time since I left my hometown in Calabria, at the age of 18, I felt home. Starting from that day on, I have been honored to be considered part of your family, and you have always made me feel like one of your sons.

I always wanted to find a way to express how much I appreciate and admire you, but sometimes it is difficult to find the right words, above all, for someone like me. One night, I drove you home from one of our

Maria, Pop's and Pietro

family reunions, and after sitting and chatting on your front porch for quite a while, I finally said, "You know, Pops, I wish one day, I will be able to look at my family and see what you have seen tonight. This is what makes a man understand that he has accomplished all that is important in life. My brothers and the family that is around you, are a pure reflection of the very special people that have made this possible, their values and their sacrifices. There isn't much more that a man can aspire to be."

We, your family, and our wonderful Country are fortunate to have you as an example to follow, and I would like you to know that I will do my best to deserve your trust and honor, being considered your fifth son.

Love your son,

*Pietro*

# A LIFE WELL LIVED

Before I start with my life, let me say how lucky I am to have the life that I have, and to be blessed with a great family. As I sit here and look back at my life, coming from a poor family, I think that it has turned out pretty good. I say poor, because back when I was born, almost everyone was poor because it was right after the depression. A lot of things have happened to me that I can't understand and I believe the Lord had something planned for me from the very beginning. Every time something happened in my life that seemed bad or unlucky, it always turned out better. There were a few of them, but I'll just tell you about a couple of them.

One, was when I met Shirley, who turned out to be my first love. We dated while in high school, but before I joined the Marines, we broke up. When I came home on an emergency leave due to my brother having cancer, I went to church one weekend and ran into Shirley — so we started dating again, and soon after we were married.

Number two was when I was in Korea. I had a couple of close calls which could have ended my life.

The third was bad. After Shirley had her open heart surgery and was doing great, she woke me up one night and told me that she was bleeding and she couldn't stop it. I called the doctor and he told me to get her to the hospital right away; they tried everything but could not save her, and two days later, she was gone. I was really bitter, but you know what, He came to my rescue once again.

This is number four. After almost two years of being alone with my two boys, I went to work one day and told the guys that I was ready to start dating. The next day, a good friend, Charlie Brown, came up to me and asked me if it was true, and said, "I've got just the lady that I think that you'll like." He told me that she had never been married and that his wife grew up with her, and that she was a good person. He couldn't believe why she hadn't gotten married by now, but maybe she hadn't met the right guy yet. Knowing Charlie and his wife, Shirley, from visiting them with Shirley, my wife, and our kids, I knew that he wouldn't steer me wrong. So, we set up a date for that next Friday, and the rest is history because she is the love of my life now and will be for the rest of our lives.

Like I said before, I am truly blessed because since the Lord saved my life in Korea, I have had two beautiful women in my life, plus six grand-children, one great grandchild, one grandson-in-law and soon one granddaughter-in-law.

This next one, happened after Marilyn and I were married, one day on the way to work. It had rained the night before and it was kind of drizzling that morning and I was going south on I-75. I had just passed over Mitchell Ave, and there wasn't any other car around me, when all at once, I started spinning around and ended up on the guard railing. Someone was tapping on my window, and asked me if I was all right and if I could get out of the car, because the gas tank has ruptured. As I got out of the car and looked up the highway, there was a semi sitting there and the driver said, "I just missed you," and I said, "Thank the Lord you did." There's more to these stories later on in my life.

I was born on Nov. 4, 1931, in a farming community, called Locust Corner, in Pierce Township, which lies between Amelia and New Richmond in Clermont County, Ohio. They named me Clyde Kenneth Eppert. My Father's name was Edgar Thomas Eppert and my Mother's maiden name was Edna May Cann. Including me, they had five children, three girls and two boys. One of my sisters, whose name was Mary Elizabeth, was born in Nov. 1926, and died that same year from the flu. Another one of my sisters, named Donna Lee, was born in Nov. 1933 and died at birth. I didn't know either one of them because one was dead before I was born, and I was too young to have known the other one. My brother's name was Edward Marion; he was born in June 1928, and he died from cancer Feb. 1953. My third sister was born on June 9, 1937. Her name was Linda Lou, and she died from cancer also. Both my father and mother died due to cancer.

Both sets of my grandparents lived in Locust Corner and they both owned farms. My mother's parents' names were John and Hattie Cann, and they had a rather large farm. Their house sat right behind the Methodist

Church on Locust Corner. My father's parents' names were Walter Moreland and Ada Eppert; their farm wasn't too far from my mother's parents' farm. They lived in a log cabin and their farm was smaller. When I was growing up, I spent a lot of time with both of them in the summer. We didn't own a farm of our own — we rented a house.

I don't remember too much about myself until my third year. It was the winter of 1934, and we moved into a house right next to the school. The school had four large rooms; each room served two classes. On one side of the room, was the first grade, and the other side was the second grade. Back then, they didn't have a kindergarten. That same year, my father became the custodian of the school. In the beginning of the school year of 1935, I was a little over three and half years old and I would go over to the school every day. One day, the principal said to my dad, "Since Ken is over here all the time, why don't you let him attend school?" I don't remember too much about that time of my life; my mom told me about me going to school. I don't remember if I stayed in first grade or what, but when we moved to the city when I was six, and my mother took my brother and me to the city school, they told my mother that I had to go to the kindergarten. They tried to move my brother back two grades but my mother said "No way," so they didn't. He was very smart, and by the time he was 18, he had two years of college. He didn't play too much with us other kids; he liked to read a lot. My mother would ask me all the time when I came home, "Why are your clothes half torn off of you, and your brother comes home looking the same as he looked when he left?" I always told mom he doesn't have any fun.

I think before I go any further, I should tell a little about my father, my mother, and my grandparents. My father was born Feb. 2, 1905, and my mother was born Jan. 8, 1909. They got married in 1925, divorced in 1942, and my mother remarried in 1943, when I was twelve, to James Switzer. By then, I was mostly paying my own way. My mother never worked too much because of my sister, so my brother and I had to work if we wanted to have any money to spend or to buy any clothes. My father remarried in 1961, to Evelyn Cox, and now I have two stepsisters and one stepbrother, two stepbrothers-in-laws and one step sister-in-law. My step sisters are Ann, who is married to Ed Geil, and Julia, who is married to Melvin Myer. My stepbrother, Eddie Clarke, married Jo Ann. Jo Ann passed away a few years ago and now it's Eddie and Martha. Eddie and I have become best of friends and are like brothers. Evelyn died in Nov. 1973. After my mom and dad got a divorce, my dad rented a room from a couple, by the names of Gus and Iola O'Banion. They lived in Walnut Hills and they became good friends. Gus was a bus driver for the city and I rode his bus when going to high school — it's a small world, isn't it? When Dad married Evelyn, they all became good friends.

Gus died a number of years later, and Iola moved back to Tennessee, where she was born, and Dad and Evelyn used to visit her all the time. After Evelyn died in 1973, Dad kept going to Tennessee and visiting Iola. They finally got married in 1975, and were married for five years, but then Dad got cancer in the brain and died in July 1980. My mother died from bone cancer in 1984. As I said before, my mother didn't work outside of the home too much; my stepfather was a stationary engineer with the William's YMCA. He got me my first real job, working in the locker room, giving out locker keys and towels; back then I made .21 cents an hour — how about that! I did this work while going to school. My father never talked too much about his work, and he didn't have a trade. I do know that after we moved to the city that he worked at different jobs, and his first job was driving a truck for a commission house, taking produce to the stores. After that, he worked at a cinder block plant, making cinder block and concrete block. When the war started, he worked at Wrights Defense Plant, which is now called G. E. After the war was over, he worked for a grocery chain, called Albers, in the warehouse. After Albers went out of business, he went to work for the Colerain School District as a custodian.

My father had one brother named Clyde Elijag. He was born in Nov. 1912, and he died in 1940. Now, you can see where I got my first name.

I would stay with him, and his wife Margaret, when I was out of school between Christmas and New Year's. I remember one year, he and I worked on model airplanes. He didn't work due to a bad heart, and that's what he died from in 1940. My mother had one sister and two brothers; her sister's name was Ann, and she died giving birth to her son, William Peter Pepper. I'll get back to him later. Her two brothers' names were Stanley and Frank. They both had left the farm when they were young. Before the war broke out, they worked with my dad at the block plant. When the war did break out, my dad was too old. My two uncles were drafted. Stanley went into the Navy and Frank went into the Army. Stan was lucky that he didn't have to go overseas, at least I don't think so. Frank did, and he fought over in Europe and was in quite a few different battles. Now, I will get back to Pete — that's what everyone called him, except for grandpa, who called him William. When Pete's mother died, they took him in, just like he was their son. When he finished school, he never left the farm like the rest of the family. He stayed and helped grandpa. After grandpa saw that Pete was going to stay, he shared everything with him, and you might say they became partners. I said before, when I was six, we moved to Cincinnati; we lived on Stites Ave. in an area called East End. Eastern Ave. was the main street; Stites Ave. was a long hill that runs from Columbia Parkway down to Eastern Ave. When it snowed in the winter time, the kids used to sled ride from the top all the way to the bottom. Back in those days, everyone heated their houses with coal; we would take the ashes and put them down at the bottom of the street to keep us from sliding out onto Eastern. In 1937, Cincinnati had a huge flood and I could look out my window and look down on Eastern, at the water covering the street. School was on Eastern, so it was closed because it was under water.

A couple years later, we moved to 4114 Eastern, and right across the street was a streetcar loop where the streetcars used to turn around. In the summertime, the school would take the kids to the zoo, so, instead of the streetcars going all the way to the end of the line, they would turn around on the loop and go back to school. Just on the other side of the loop, was a street that took you to Lunken Airport. This is where all the airlines flew out, before Greater Cincinnati Airport opened up years later. Beyond that street, was an open lot that used to be an old glass works factory, and you know how kids are, a place to play right? — wrong! One day, when we were playing, I was barefoot, so naturally I stepped on a piece of glass and cut my foot pretty bad. The rest of the kids carried me home because I couldn't walk. When they got me home, my foot was bleeding a lot, so my dad put ice on it to stop the bleeding. He took me to one doctor's office, who told my dad to take me to the hospital because he said I needed stitches to close the cut up. My dad didn't think I needed stitches, so we went to another doctor and all he did was put a bandage over the cut. Wouldn't you know it; that was the week school was going to the zoo, so I just sat on my porch and cried, watching the streetcars making the turn on the loop to go by school to pick up the kids.

The next year after I was stuck in the third grade was the year that World War II broke out, Dec. 7, 1941, when Japan bombed Pearl Harbor. That same year, my dad went to Patterson, New Jersey, for training in a defense plant here in Cincy, called Wrights, which today is GE. I spent that same year with Grandma and Grandpa Cann and took my third grade over. The last day of school, my Grandma died in her sleep and it was quite a shock to all of us because she wasn't even sick. That summer, I spent with my great uncles and aunts in Kentucky — they also had farms. It was funny that my grandparents used horses to work their farms, but even though my uncles had horses they did their work with tractors. When I came home the next time, I saw my Grandpa Cann and asked him, "How come you don't use a tractor on your farm?" He said, "We can't use a tractor because our land is too hilly." Then, I said, "What do mean too hilly? They have more hills than you have." They finally got one and my Granddad said to me, "I should have listened to you a long time ago because it sure made farming a lot easier."

* * *

As you know, Cincinnati is close to the Ohio River, since I told you about the flood in 1937. After we moved up on Eastern, we had other floods but we were up high enough that it didn't reach us. Lunken Airport was lower and they got flooded every once in a while. They even built dikes around the airport but they didn't keep the water out all the time.

Since our houses were so close together, we didn't have many places to play, we just had a small strip of dirt next to our house. We did have a small woods in the back of our house, and as far as we knew, no one owned them, so, we used to build forts and play cowboys and Indians. Down by the airport, there was a big field where we used to play football. I still have a scar on my right hand from falling on stubble. We used to fly kites off the dikes. In the summertime, we would collect wood and take it down there, and in the winter we would burn it to keep warm when we sledded off of the dikes.

When my brother, Marion, was going to high school, he worked at the airport, putting food on the planes for the passengers — this is how he earned money for college. He also got into a program at U.C., that they called, "V5;" he was to take two years of college, then go to Pensacola Naval Air Force training station to become a pilot. After he went through the schooling and started the flying part, he couldn't cut it. He had trouble with making landings, so, he washed out. He always said he wanted to be a doctor, so, when he came home, he went back to school, but for some reason that didn't work out either. So, he got a job with P. & G. as an assistant chemist, working with foods for animals. He used to go in on Saturday and feed them and clean up after them. One day, he was moving some barrels, and one of them slipped out of his grip and bumped him in the chest. He didn't think too much about it, but it ended up turning into cancer, and in turn causing his death at the age of 24. He got married when he was 20, to Frances Green, and they had a boy by the name of James Edward; but everyone in the family called him Jay. He was only two years old when Marion died. Jay's mother remarried a few years later and had two girls. When Jay got older, he moved to

Wisconsin and got married, and as far as I know, has one child, but, then, he just disappeared. I haven't heard anything from him in a few years.

I also did some work at the airport on the weekends, when I was 11 or 12, selling popcorn, pop, and ice cream bars to the people that would watch the planes land and take off.

Here is another thing that I forgot to tell you, and that is Lunken Airport is where all the passenger planes landed, because Greater Cincinnati airport wasn't built until years later. In those days, we didn't have Cinergy Ballpark or Kings Island Amusement Park, but we did have Crosley Field Ballpark and Coney Island Amusement Park. Coney was right on the river and there was a boat called the Island Queen Ferry. It was a big paddle wheel boat that would take you from the dock at Cincy to the dock at Coney. You could go to Coney by the boat or bus and neither of them cost a lot to ride. Then, one day, the Island Queen caught on fire, and it was too far gone, so, then, you had to ride the bus to get there. Coney was like Kings Island, but on a smaller scale; one thing it had, and still has, is one of the largest fresh water swimming pools in the world.

• • •

After I was married and the kids got a little older, my dad and the kids and I would go down to Crosley Field and watch the Reds play. When I was younger, I used to go when it was knot-hole day, which was usually on Saturdays. I remember, one day, a bunch of us went bowling up at 20 Century Bowling Alley and we happened to look over a couple of lanes. We recognized a couple of the Reds players; one was first baseman Big Klu., and Grady Hatten, with their wives. Big Klu. had arms as big as my thighs. I can't remember how he spelled his last name but everyone just called him Big Klu.

When school let out for the summer, I would stay with my grandparents because I loved the farm. I always said I wanted to be a farmer when I grew up but it never happened. I spent most of my summers with Grandpa Cann and Pete after he got married. They raised different kinds of crops, like tomatoes, string beans, potatoes, apples, and blackberries, which they took to the farmers' market. Grandpa would hire a lot of the neighbor's kids and mothers to help pick them.

He paid them so much a quart for the berries, so much per bushel for beans; these crops were the hardest to pick and also time consuming. Pete and Grandpa picked and graded the apples, the same with the tomatoes. They would plow up the potatoes and I would follow behind and pick them up. At the end of the day, we would put them on the truck and take them to the farmers' market in Cincy to sell. If you were lucky, and your tomatoes got ripe before anyone else, you made good money. That's why you staked them, so that the sun got to them easier and they would ripen faster. That was one of my jobs, tying up the tomatoes to the stakes, 400 of them. When you got to market, there were other farmers there also trying to sell their produce, and sometimes, you were there overnight. Sometimes, you got lucky, one of the produce commission houses would buy all of your produce and you got to go home early. I'll never forget the time we sold out early. Pete said to me, "Let's go get something to eat." You won't believe this, but that's when I got introduced to White Castle some 60 odd years ago.

One of the other crops they raised was tobacco, which was a big money crop back then. Back then, you had to be in the tobacco patch almost every day because of the worms, weeds and you had to pull the suckers off. Those were the little shoots that grow up between the stock and the leaf and after they are full grown, you have to break the top off, before it turns into a flower, and then into seed. Like I said, they had horses, so they raised hay to feed in the winter. They milked a lot of cows and sold it to a CO-OP to make money; they raised hogs to sell at market and also to eat; and chickens to eat and sell the eggs. With all of these animals, they grew corn to feed them. Most farms have cats living on them, so when we milked the cows, the cats would come around begging for milk. We used to squirt them in the mouth with it. Grandpa and Pete taught me how to do everything on the farm, I mean everything, from soup to nuts. They rotated their crops, so when I got older and had a garden, I rotated everything that I planted.

One day, I was on a field raking hay with a horse, by the name of Tom. A big, black racer snake crossed in front of us and startled him, and he took off on me, like a scared rabbit. It took all my strength to stop him. When we put the hay in the barn, I used to ride Tom. Grandpa had a big pitchfork hanging from a rope, that was attached to a pulley, that hooked to a beam, higher up. Grandpa would back the wagon that was full of hay into the barn, unhook the team of horses and take them away, then hook Tom up to the other end of the rope that held the pitchfork. Then, he would stick the fork into the hay and then say, "OK Ken, take Tom forward," which would lift the fork up over the hay loft. He then, would pull another rope, which released the hay from the fork and let it drop into the loft.

This same barn was full of rafters that were used for hanging tobacco on. You see, when Grandpa and Pete cut the tobacco, they would put the stocks on sticks and then hang the sticks over the rafters. During the fall season, the tobacco would cure and then they stripped the leaves from the stocks and put them into bundles. Then, they would take the tobacco to the warehouses and sell it. At that time, tobacco was a big money crop for farmers. I used to climb up into the rafters and dive into the hay loft. One day, I was playing in the barn, climbing around on the rafters and ran into a nest of wasps, and got stung five times. By the time I got to the house, I could hardly see, because my eyes had swollen so much, and that taught me a good lesson about not climbing around in the barn.

My Grandpa and Grandma Eppert had a couple cows and a lot of chickens. Grandma made butter out of the excess milk and sold it. They had just a few chickens for eggs for themselves; the rest they sold to someone who would come pick them up and take them away to a meat packing company to kill and package them and put in stores to sell. Their farm was close to where mound-dwelling Native Americans lived years ago. Every time Grandpa would plow a field, he would find arrow-heads and other things that belonged to the Native Americans. When they got older, they sold the farm and bought a house in Amelia, where they still raised a big garden. Grandma used to put up pickled beets for me because I liked them so much. I forgot to tell you, that on the farm, they lived in a log cabin with a lot of rooms added on. They had a wind-up Victor record player that I would play every time I had the chance, and I wish that I had taken it when I had the chance.

When they got too old to take care of themselves, they moved to a nursing home, and Dad said to me to take anything that I wanted. Grandpa put those arrow-heads in a case and as you know, I have that case. My great grandfather was in the Civil War. His name was Walter Butler Eppert and he was in A Company, 34th Regiment, Ohio Volunteer Infantry or Pratt's Zouaves. He went in on the 27th of July, 1861, as a private. He was honorably discharged on the 27 July, 1865, and served as Commander and Past Commander of G. W. Robinson Post No. 487 Department of Ohio. So, as you all know, I also have a case of things from the Civil War.

Now that the history class is over, let's get back to my life. All through grade school, I just got through by the skin of my teeth. The only classes I liked were math and art. I always got high grades in those classes. When the war broke out in 1941, the school sold war bond stamps to put in a book, and when you got the book full, you turned it in for a War Bond. My math teacher appointed me and a girl in my class to go around to all the other grades and collect the money for the stamps.

Our school yard was covered with blacktop. It was real smooth, so we used to roller skate on it. We also used to play hockey on it, but if you fell down, you got pretty scuffed up. I would come home with my pants torn at the knees and have bruises on my knees and legs.

We moved to Walnut Hills when I was in the eighth grade, and that's when I was introduced to the black race of people. Don't get me wrong I knew of them, but never had any dealings with them, as far as being in school with them or living in the same neighborhood. I didn't think differently toward them, because they looked just like me, only they were black. Walnut Hills back then was sort of divided into two sections, with the borderline being Woodburn Ave. On one side, the blacks lived and the other the whites lived. There were quite a few at my new school and there never were any problems between us kids.

Back then, teachers asked us what we thought we wanted to do with our lives. I said I wanted to be a farmer, machinist or a carpenter, since I liked to do things with my hands. Back then, you either went to a regular high school or a vocational one. Since I knew I probably couldn't afford to go to college, I chose to go to Central Vocational High. The first two years, each semester, you took different types of shop classes for a half day, and the rest of the day you took regular classes. The last two years, you took the shop classes that you wanted to work at when you graduated. My freshman year, I had machine and electric shops, along with algebra, English, science, gym and music. My sophomore year, I had geometry, world history, English, gym and music, along with wood and mechanical drawing shops. Since I liked machine shop so much, I decided to take it my last two years. We had shop all morning, and took the other classes in the afternoon. I had trigonometry for two years. My junior year, I took American history, English, music and gym; and, my senior year I took English, advanced mechanical drawing, gym and music. During my years in high school, I did some other things, but since I worked most of the time after school, I couldn't do a lot. Another reason, was when I was born, one of my testicles stayed up in my groin, and they tried different medicines but nothing worked, so the doctor said wait until I was a teenager to have it operated on. So, when I was 15, the doctor operated on me and brought it down and stitched it to my leg, so that's why I couldn't play any contact sports. You know how they do things now — sometimes you're in and out the same day — but I was in the hospital bed for three weeks before they even let me out of the bed. It was stitched there for several months so it could heal, so I couldn't even take gym.

Between my sophomore and junior years, in the summertime, football practice started two weeks before school. I became a team manager.

We gave out equipment and took water out on the field during practice. After the team started playing games, I was the one up in booth, telling the person who was doing play-by-play, who made the tackles, and who was carrying the ball for our team. Since we didn't have a gym at school, we took gym classes at the same place we practiced football, which was called Deer Creek Commons. Our school was on Item Street, which ran down from McMillan, and the gym and practice field were down on Gilbert Ave. So, when we went to gym, we either walked or rode a school bus — if it was running at the time.

I forgot to tell you what happened that summer at practice; before school starts in the fall, the high schools practice for two weeks. We used to practice all day, so during the noon break, another one of the managers and I went across the street for lunch at this little bar. You see, back then, most of the bars had pinball machines, and even though it was against the law, if you happened to hit for games, you could get money for them. After I ate my lunch, I walked over to one of them, put money in and proceeded to hit it for some games. These two guys were at the bar eating, and we didn't know who they were when we walked into the bar. When I asked the lady bartender for my money, these guys pulled out their badges and said, "You are under arrest."

Needless to say I was shocked and scared at the same time. They padlocked the bar, put us in the car, and took us to the station. They put the bartender in jail right then and started asking us questions. They asked if this was our first time there at that bar; it was my first but Chaney said he had eaten there last year because he was a manager then also. Like I said before, I really was scared. I was only 17 at the time, Chaney was 18. Well, we found out later that they just wanted us as material witnesses and to testify against the bartender. We went to court several times, but they kept continuing the case, and we kept asking the officers what's going on, and they finally told us we didn't have to appear any more. I'll never forget this one time, while we were in court, this one black guy was up in front of the Judge. He said to this man, "I'm going to put you on a bus and I never want to see your black ass in front of me again." At that same time, I was helping my two uncles on Saturdays, who were partners in building houses up in Withamsville. I used to ride the bus every Saturday to get there.

* * *

It's funny — you remember I said I just got through grade school by the skin of my teeth. Well, I really took to high school for some reason or another. I ended up being sixth in my class when I graduated out of around 250 boys (our school was all male). I think my two lowest grades were 75's on two exams, both English. As I said before, I always got the top grade in math, but in high school, the teachers never gave out 100's, I always got 98. In fact, I was so good in trig that when the teacher put a problem on the board, I would get the answer right away. Some of the guys would ask the teacher a question about the problem, and he would tell them to go see Eppert — "he can tell you how to do it."

The year after my mother remarried, we moved to Walnut Hills; I was in the 8th grade. We lived on the corner of Hackberry Ave and De Sales Lane. When I turned 14, I worked at different jobs. One was at the YMCA. I worked at a neighborhood grocery store stocking the shelves and delivering groceries to people who called in orders. While working there, I also helped in the butcher shop, and learned a little about cutting meat. When I turned 15, I got a job working at the RKO Shubert Theater downtown, as an usher. I lied about my age because you had to be 16 before you could work for them. I always looked older than I was, so they believed me when I told them I was 16. One night, the manager called me into the office, and he said to me, "I want you to find me this certain Florida paper." This is how I found my way around the town of Cincy, because I walked all over trying to find this paper, which I never did. I think the manager was playing a joke on me.

I think I told you before that between my junior and senior year, we stayed in school the whole time. Since I was the top guy in the machine shop, myself and another guy, by the name of Rudy, got jobs at a tool and dye shop, called "Panda Products." We started in August 1949, and we would go to school for two weeks and go to work for two weeks. While I was at work, he was in school, and when I was in school, he worked. We made 65 cents an hour, and after we graduated they gave us a raise to 90 cents. When I started working at Panda, they had a fast-pitch softball team and asked me if I would like to play. I played first base and the outfield sometimes. We played our games at the same place that we took our gym classes at high school. I remember while we were playing a game one night, the guy that was playing center field all at once disappeared, not knowing that there was a hole out there he fell into it. Luck was with him, because he didn't get hurt. Another time, a guy by the name of Erv. Hoffman, who was our second baseman, jammed his middle finger pretty bad. This same fellow was a Navy Reservist, so when Korea broke out, he got orders to return to the Navy. You talk about a mad guy! He was really mad and he said that they would pay for calling him back. There's more on him later on in my life.

• • •

I've got a head of myself a little bit. I started dating in my junior year, because I didn't have too much money before then. After we moved to Walnut Hills, I started going to Bethlehem Methodist Church on Woodburn Ave. to Sunday school. On Sunday evenings, we used to go back to church for activities. One night, I met a young girl by the name of Shirley Jamison; she was a year younger than me. We dated off and on for a couple years, and then we broke up for one reason or another. Shirley's mother died when she was 13 years old. They lived in Indiana at the time, and her father had died a few years before. Her sister, Dorothy, with her husband, George Lowenstine, lived on Spokane Ave. in Walnut Hills. They didn't have any children of their own. George had a daughter from a previous marriage, so they brought Shirley to live with them. I'm sorry I've got ahead of myself again — before she went to live with her sister, she stayed with a brother in Indiana. I was told that he worked her pretty hard and she came down with rheumatic fever, so Dorothy and George got her and took her home to live with them. There's more to this story later.

The year I graduated was June 1950. Shirley, me, Dorothy and George were visiting George's daughter's family. We were reading the paper and I read where North Korea attacked South Korea. So, since we had troops there, we went to war against North Korea. Sometime after that, Shirley and I broke up, so I started dating other girls. While going to work in Nov. of that year, a friend of mine was on the bus already and we got to talking about different things. One thing led to another and all at once he says to me, "Let's join the Marines." I said, "Are you serious?" and he says, "Yes," so, we decided then to go and sign up. When we got to town, we walked into the Marine recruiting office and joined. I went home and then when I walked in the house, Mom said to me, "What are you doing home so soon?" All I said was, "I just joined the Marines." She couldn't say too much because at that time I was already 19, and I didn't need her consent. We had a couple of days before we had to report, so the next day I told them at work. I told them that I knew that I would probably be called up pretty soon and that I wanted to be in an outfit that took care of their people, so that's the reason I joined the Marines.

So off Don and I went to Paris Island, South Carolina, to boot camp. On the train, we met a couple guys from Dayton, Ohio, by the names of Fred Shedden and Bob (I can't remember his last name). I was not used to hearing foul language, but as soon as we pulled into the station, this Sgt. jumped on and said the "F" word and told us to get off the train. From then on, we got our wake-up call; we were lucky the four of us were put in the same company. When we got to our barracks, our Drill Instructor was waiting for us, and his name was Sgt. Service. You could tell right away that he was going to be tough, by the way he talked. The first thing we did was get our heads shaved, and from there we were taken to our Barracks. We were then given two sheets, a pillow, pillow case and a blanket. From there, we were taken to the place to get our uniforms and other clothes. We got two pairs of dress trousers, five sets of khakis, one pair of dress shoes, one pair boon-docker shoes, seven pairs of socks, seven tee shirts, seven pair of jockey shorts, two sets of dungarees, two dungaree caps, a field jacket, one Ike jacket and a cap (I can't remember what they were called), and a large duffel bag to put your clothes in when you traveled. Then, we were issued our M1, with our other equipment, cartridge belt, first aid kit, bayonet, canteen — all three of these hung from your cartridge belt — poncho, half of a pup tent, tent pegs, sleeping bag, tent pole, and a mess kit. You carried all these things in your backpack, which was called a haversack, along with a small shovel. When broken down, by this I mean the blade would close down on the handle, then it would fit into a holder on the haversack. All of this equipment stayed with you wherever you went, including your blanket.

We were there for only eight weeks, so you see why the D. I. had to be so tough — they had to take the civilian out of you and make you Marines. The first six weeks, all you did was march, run double time anywhere you went, and do different movements with your rifle when you were marching. You also did a lot of calisthenics to tone your muscles and get your whole body in shape. You also took aptitude tests, which I did well in. You were given a book, called the *Marine Corps Manual* that you had to read that told the do's and don't's and other things that were expected of you. As in anything you do, you have some good times and some bad ones.

Don was always complaining that he didn't do too well; I think it was more than he expected it to be. I went into it with a clear mind, kept my shoes spit shined and uniforms clean and neat, and myself neat and clean. Our D. I. had these things on his boots, that made a noise when he walked, like this "clink, clink." One day, we were marching to chow, and we always marched three abreast. Freddy and I were in one of the outside lines; he was two guys in front of me. The guy between us was always messing up, so this time, he decides to mess up, and all of a sudden the D. I. says, "Company, Halt." Then here comes, "clink, clink," and you knew right then that someone was going to catch hell. He kept getting closer and closer, I kind of noticed Freddy shaking a little bit, but he wasn't after him. He grabbed the guy between us, threw him on the ground and stomped on him. This happened two days in a row; the guy's name was Gridry, and he was from Louisiana.

The seventh week, we went to the rifle range. That week, all you did was practice the four positions of how you fired your rifle; they call that "snapping in." The four positions are prone, kneeling, setting and offhand. Here's a couple of funny things that happened while we were out there. When we were snapping in that first week, Freddy developed a case of the GI's, and in the middle of one night, I woke up from this loud bang and I heard Freddy yell. You see, while we were out there, we stayed in Quonset Huts, which were steel, so the door was steel and that caused the big bang when he shut it. We didn't have a latrine in our hut — there was one big latrine everyone used, so you see, he didn't make it to the latrine in time. So, we gave Fred the nick name of Shitty Sheddon. The latrine was one long bench with a lot of holes in it, and once in a while, guys would catch someone sitting on one end and reading something or not paying attention. They would wad up a lot of paper and light it and let it float down on the water that ran down the trough under him. Well sometimes they wouldn't have time to wipe and had to get up and run out. Anything for a laugh!

Now, we get to the Rifle Range — the 8th week we started firing on the range. The first day, we fired from 100 yards, and first of all, we started from the prone position. You got down in position, lined the target in your sight, took a deep breath, let it out slow and squeezed the trigger. If you were lucky and hit the target, but missed left or right of the bull's eye, there was a little knob above and in front of the stock of your rifle to make corrections. You kept this up until you hit the center of the bull, then you wrote down on a piece of paper how many clicks you moved that knob. Once you did that, you moved back to 500 yards and did the same thing because the wind will change the direction of a bullet. After you have your rifle zeroed in, you practice firing from the other three positions. The day before we qualified was perfect — not much wind and no clouds, and you always fired a practice round before you qualified. A perfect score is 240, and that's all bulls' eyes. The target was a five-foot square piece of heavy paper that was on a mechanism that pulled up and down. The target had three rings and a black bull's eye that was 8" in diameter. Bull's eye was 10 points, between the bull and the first ring was 9 then 8 then 7; if you hit outside the target, you got a white flag and 5 points, if you then missed it all together, you got a red flag which was called "maggie's drawers." I really shot good that day and got a score of 232 which is Expert. Well, the next day was horrible. It was cloudy and foggy with a light drizzle, so I didn't shoot so good. I shot a 192, which still qualified me as a marksman. If you shot less than marksman, you had to do it over. Everyone in the Corps is a rifleman first and then given a different duty later.

After graduation, we got a 10 day leave; it was late Dec. and we were getting letters from home that they were getting a lot of snow. When I got home, the snow was all gone. Our orders said for us to report back to Paris Island until they had enough people to fill a troop train up to send to California for advanced training. I can't remember how many men there were but the train was very long. On the way, we made several stops so that we could get out and stretch; it took us two days to get through the desert alone. One stop was in Douglas, Arizona, and we made two stops in Texas, Houston and Dallas. It took us five days to get there; they loaded us on buses and drove us to Camp Pendleton Marine Corps Base, near the coast of the Pacific Ocean. Our area was called Tent Camp, and when you went out the back gate, you were on Highway One. If you went to the right, it took you to Los Angeles, if you went to the left it took you to San Diego.

I forgot to tell you, that Fred, Don and me stayed together. Bob got different orders and stayed at Paris Island for reassignment. Since he knew how to type, he was going to be a Remington Raider. That's the name they gave guys that worked in the offices.

When we got to Tent Camp, we were all assigned to Weapons Co. We were not in tents, but were put into the kind of Quonset Huts that we had at the rifle range. Like I said before, the three to us stayed together. The first day we were there, the Sgt. in charge of our Company said we had our choice of what we wanted to do. Weapons Co. is made up of different Weaponry — Machine Guns, 60mm Mortars, Antitank Tank Guns, Flame Throwers, 75mm Recoilless Rifle and Bazookas. Fred and I chose 60 Mortars, and Don took Machine Guns. Due to the good test scores I got when I enlisted, they made me a Section Leader. We did a lot of field trips to get you used to carrying all of your personal equipment. You had a back pack, called a haversack, that carried your extra clothes, another pair of socks, skivvies, change of dungarees, half of a tent and tent pegs, sleeping bag which you tied on top of the haversack, extra boon-dockers, that's what we called our shoes, and all of your toiletries. We practiced setting up the 60's and simulated firing missions, then one day we did some firing with live ammo. Sorry, I didn't tell you what a Mortar was or what it did — it's a short barreled cannon with a low muzzle velocity, which hurls shells in a high trajectory. It's not like artillery shells, that make a whistling noise as soon as it leaves the gun. When a mortar leaves the tube, it doesn't make noise until it's just about to hit the ground. Therefore, it's too late to duck before it hits. There are three kinds of Mortars: 60's, 81's and 4.2's, the last two are much larger and have longer ranges. The 60 has three components but they are attached together, where the other two have three separate parts. They all have a tripod, tube and a base plate.

When Fred went home after boot camp, he got married, and she came out to California to be with Fred, because she knew he would be going overseas after his advanced training. She stayed at a town called Ocean Side, which was just outside of tent camp on Highway One. Not too long after she came out, Fred's sister came out to visit and I ended up dating her. It was right after Easter when we shipped out, but on Easter Sunday, Fred's wife and his sister fixed dinner for us.

Right after that, they loaded 3,000 of us on buses and took us to San Diego, so that we could board two ships, 1500 on each APA Ship. Guess what? I got seasick before we left the dock, but it didn't last long. Right after we pulled out, I happened to have a Baby Ruth candy bar in my haversack, so I ate it and I didn't get sick again. Boy, was I glad, because we had a rough voyage! It took us 23 days to get to Kobe, Japan. We hit a storm one day and it was so bad that we only went 8 miles in a 24 hour period. It was hard to eat sometimes, because you had a hard time keeping your tray in front of you while you ate. The waves were so high that when we looked over at the other ship, you thought that it must have sunk because it was gone behind the wave. After the 24 days, we finally got to Kobe, and we were so glad to get off that ship, that we liked to have torn that town up. There were guys so messed up that they were trying to get rickshaws up the gangway of the ship. We were so long on the trip that the only thing we had to eat were Vienna sausages, and I can't look at one today without getting sick.

Before I go any further, let me give you the nomenclature of a Division of the Marine Corps. It's divided up into threes. A Division has three Regiments, each Reg. has three Battalions, each Batt. has three Companies, each Com. has three Platoons, each Plat. has three Sections, each Sec. has three Squads, each Sq. has three Fire Teams and each Fire Team has four men — a Leader, BAR Man, Rifle Man and an Ammo Carrier. They also have Headquarters, Supply and Weapons Company, Motor Pool, 4.2 Company, Light artillery 105's, Heavy artillery 155's along with Tanks. All in all about 18,000 troops.

When we got there, it was already dark, so they put me and the other guys with the H and S Company. These guys are the Remington Raiders of the Battalion. Let me tell you, I was a little nervous that night. In the morning after we were up, they took the first six that had taken 60 mortars at Pendleton. I happened to be one them, and they told us, "You're going to the 81's." Fred and Don went to the Line Companies, but I got lucky and ended up in Weapons Co. 2nd Battalion 7th. Each Battalion has three Line Co's. and one Weapons Co. and each Line Co. has three platoons. The Weapons Co. has three sections of 81's, three guns in each. I was put into the second section, which backed up Dog, Easy and Fox Co. When I got to my section, a couple guys came over and introduced themselves. There were two guys standing in the mortar pit after I joined them, and one of them handed me this grenade. He said, "Look at it and tell me what it says." I looked at it and saw the initials M.T. inscribed on the side of it, and handed it back to him. He took it, and proceeded to pull the pin and let it drop. I knew what a grenade was, because we had training with them at Pendleton. So, I just went over backwards out of the hole and looked up, and they were laughing. He said, "Didn't you read that the M. T. means empty?" After that, we became good friends.

As usual, I've gotten ahead of myself. I haven't told you how the Marines got involved in the war. They didn't call it a war, they said it was a Police Action — don't kid yourself, it was a War. If I'm not mistaken, we had more casualties in Korea than any other War. At the time when the North attacked, we only had Army personnel there and they were poorly trained and equipped. Since it had been only 4 years after WWII was over, the Korean Army hadn't had a chance to get up to power either. It didn't take long for the North to push our people from the 38th parallel which was the dividing point of the two countries. Before we could fully equip our troops, they had our people pushed almost to Puson. At that time, General MacArthur was the Supreme Commander of the Eastern Theater. In Sept. of 1950 he asked and got the 1st' Division of the Marines to make an amphibious landing at a place called Inch'on, so we could cut off the North's supply lines. When this happened, the Southern troops started pushing the North again, and trapped and captured a lot of the North Koreans, and everyone started saying the War would be over by Christmas. Well, that didn't work out because the Chinese stepped in. After the Marines landed at Inch'on, which was still in South Korea near Seoul, and everything went well, MacArthur decided that he wanted the Marines to make another landing in North Korea, on the west coast at a town called Wonsan.

There were other troops fighting north on the eastern part, so he wanted the Marines, after they landed, to swing east and join up with other troops swinging west, therefore, cutting off the escaping enemy. During this time, the Chinese Communist Troops were building up along the border in Manchuria. Every time, MacArthur was told that the C.C.F. was putting more troops on the border. He always said that they won't come across the border, but of course he ended up being wrong. After the 1st Marine guaranteed the safety of Monsoon, they sent my 7th Bat. north to the Chosin Reservoir, then to the Yalu River, west of the 7th Division forces. This area was very rough, mountains 7,000 to 8,000 feet high, and roads were nothing but cow paths. Having received word of the massive C.C.F. attack on the 8th Cav. at Unsan, they were told to go forward with caution. Shortly after midnight, Nov. 3rd, the C.C.F. 124th Div. swarmed into the 7th, blowing whistles and horns. At first, they got the upper hand, but when daylight came, they got Marine artillery and close air support. It inflicted a punishing slaughter on them, some 700 dead and thousands wounded.

The fight continued on and off for the next three days, then suddenly on Nov. 7th, they disappeared. Our guys figured they retreated because they had so many casualties. As it turned out, that was the reason. We figured that they had around 7,000 casualties, but we just had 314. There were other battles fought with C.C.F. all along the North, and it seemed more C.C.F. troops were showing up, but then they seemed to disappear again. When the Marines started north again, here came the C.C.F. again, but this time, they estimated there were 200,000 of them so then everyone started withdrawing. One of the newsmen asked General O. P. SMITH of the 1st Div. Marines if he was retreating and he said, "Hell no, we're just attacking in a different direction." I got most of this information from a book I have entitled, *The Forgotten War*, that's all about Korea. It's here if you would like to read it. As I was reading this same book myself, about when my Batt. was moving back south after the C.C.F. attacked the second time, my squad leader's name popped up. His name was

O'Leary, and when I got there, I heard a lot of stories about the things he did with the 81 when they were retreating south. The Gooks were so close behind them that he was shooting the 81 almost straight up, which is a no-no with the 81.

Let me explain an 81 mortar. You have three separate parts when broken down. The main piece is the tripod, which weighs 45 lbs. When you're moving out, you carry it on your shoulder. It sounds like a lot of weight but when I got there, most of the guys had what they called back packs. It was made of a real hard material with shoulder straps and when you put it on, the back stuck above your shoulders, so when you are carrying the tripod, it's resting on the back pack. The same with the tube, which weighs 45 lbs. also, and you carry it on your shoulder. The last part, the base plate, is carried a little different. You have to carry it with both hands in front of you, with the back resting on your belt. This thing weighs 47 lbs., so you see, the base plate man has the hardest job if you have to carry it for a long distance. The longest range for it is about 2,000 yards, so when Dog and Easy moved, we had to follow them.

Korea is a pretty rough country made of mountains, valleys and rice paddies. When we would run into the people away from towns, you would see a house, every once in a while. When you did see a house, it wouldn't be very big, and there would be 20 or more people coming out of it, we always wondered — where did they sleep? The weather was about the same as ours when I got there. It got hotter as the months passed, with a lot of rain. The first of Sept., it started getting cooler.

After I got to my Company, the next day, the whole Battalion headed out on a mission called Operation Mouse Trap. We went 15 miles in front of our own lines, and set up a 360 degree perimeter. The reason we did this was because the higher ups said there was a lot of the enemy farther out in front of us. We were supposed to be bait to try to suck them into falling back into a fortified position behind us. Well, we were out there for three weeks and nothing happened, until the last night we were there. I had gun watch that night. The evening before, some of the line troops started moving back to our main lines with lights on their trucks and making a lot of noise. At about 4 in the morning, all hell broke loose across the valley from us. I heard a lot of machine gun fire and saw some jets dropping napalm. I couldn't see what the jets were dropping the napalm on, or what they were shooting at. When daylight came, there was a call for a section of 81's to come forward, so it took off, with me. I said to myself, this will be a way to find out how I would react when I saw my first dead enemy. I was very much surprised, because it didn't bother me at all. When we got there, they were already bulldozing them into a big hole. They figured there were about 500 of them, and it looked like they were new people because their uniforms were new and they said every one of them had a new fountain pen.

After we were there for a while, I ran into a friend of mine and he told me what had happened. He said that after he got his heavy machine gun set up, after they stopped for the night, everyone sacked out except for the ones on watch. He said he was awakened by bugles blowing and the beating of drums. He knew it had to be the enemy because he had heard that they did things like that. So, he jumped out of his sleeping bag and got on his gun and saw them coming at 8 abreast, toward them, blowing bugles and beating drums. He said when he saw this, he just turned the gun on them and mowed them down. Nobody could figure out why they didn't attack us while we were moving back instead of waiting until we got set up. Oh, I forgot to say that these people were Chinese Communist Troops.

The Gooks, that's what we called them, had every place there zeroed in with their mortars and artillery. The reason for this, was that before WWII, the Japanese had already invaded Korea, and they had plotted the country then and still had their maps from then. That's the reason we had troops there when North Korea attacked the South. That's also the reason we never went up the middle of a valley when we came to one. We always stayed close to the edges. This one time, we had just got our guns set up and in place, when this replacement group started right up the middle of the valley. Well, we started getting a lot of incoming, by this I mean mortar and artillery shells dropping all around us. I hadn't had time to dig my fox hole, so I laid in this little gully and climbed inside my helmet. Luck was with us — a lot of the shells were duds. We had one person get hit by shrapnel, from a piece of steel from our Jeep that was hit by a shell. Runt Owens, he was hit in the shoulder, and since his year was almost up, he didn't come back. We got a letter from him sometime later; you see, he was with the guys that landed at Inch'on. After they landed, they hit them so hard that they overran them, and doing this caused the Gooks to drop their weapons and run. So, Runt had a Russian 31 caliber rifle, a Japanese Long Tom Rifle and some other things, along with an animal skin of some varmint he had killed. That was the only thing he had trouble getting through Customs going home. I have another funny story to tell you about Runt before he got wounded and left. I'll get to it later.

Like I said before, in the summer it was hot and we had a lot of rain. I guess that's why they could raise rice. The roads were nothing but dirt, so most of the time we were walking in mud up to our ankles. For about a week straight we were in the rain. Every time we stopped and got set up, we would get orders to move out again, this got old after a while. I remember after we had been on front lines awhile, we went into reserves. It had quit raining the day before. That night I had guard duty. and don't you know, it started raining, and I mean really hard. To my surprise, when I got back to my tent, everything was floating. Needless to say I didn't get much sleep that night.

Now, let's get back to that funny story about Runt. At that time, I had made base plate Man. We had to follow our Line Company that went out on patrol, and we had gone quite a ways, when all at once, we started getting some incoming fire. The Lieutenant yelled, "Let's get out of here!" Well, here I am carrying this base plate and I look up, and here's Runt laying on the ground. He's yelling "Help me, help me, I can't get up." Like I said before, he's got all this weight from the other gear he's carrying, so he can't get up. I couldn't help from laughing, so I dropped the base plate and helped him up.

One time, when we were in reserves, I went looking for Freddy, who was in the 3rd Battalion 7th. Remember the problem he had at the rifle range in boot camp? As soon as I saw him, he said he still had the GI's. I said, "You're kidding," and he said he wasn't, "They've tried everything, and the problems are still there, not as bad, but I've still got them." Then, I asked if he had seen Don, lately. You remember me saying that he wasn't cut out to be a Marine. He went to a line company, since he was in machine guns. He complained so much that one day the guy in front of him who was carrying the gun dropped it and it landed on Don's foot and broke it.

The guy that dropped it told Fred he got tired of Don complaining so much that he thought it was a good way to get rid of him. I don't know what ever happened to him because I have not run across him since.

I'm sorry for jumping around like this, but as I'm writing, I keep remembering other funny things that happened at boot camp. There was another fellow in our platoon at Boot Camp that had been a Prisoner Of War during WWII. He was kind of messed up from being a prisoner because of some of the things he did. One day, when the D. I. was teaching us the nomenclature of the M1 rifle, all at once he says, "What do you do when you have to go the bathroom?" One day, at the rifle range, snapping in, he started making noises like a whistle of a train and clucking like a chicken. The D. I. caught him and made him go all over the range making those noises. By the way, after the D.I. explained the nomenclature of the rifle, we had to practice field stripping it until we could take it apart and put it back together blind folded.

We had a firing mission one day while backing our line company. We pumped so many rounds out, that we could have fried eggs on the base plate. We almost fired a whole truckload, but then some days we wouldn't fire one round. On pushing the Gooks so hard, we started picking up some of their gear. One of the Heavy Machine Gun Sections found one of their horses. He was a good looking horse, so we figured he must have been an officer's horse. He stayed with us. Not too long after that, we came to a place that was like a cliff, and we had just enough room to walk across. When we started across we became aware that we were under fire from small arms, so we pulled back and waited for nightfall. Once we started across, it got pretty scary because some of the places were pretty narrow, but you know what, the next morning that horse was on the other side with us!

I had some close calls myself, like the day that Runt Owns got hit. Another time, we had just set up our guns on this plateau and I had just finished digging my foxhole. Down below, there was a group of South Korean civilians picking up chow to take up to the Line Companies. Right about then, a 120mm mortar round came down right in the middle of them. There must have been 30 of them. The good part about it was that only one was hurt. As they were taking him to the aid station just below us, three guys from my company went running past me to see how the guy was that got hurt. I was just about to climb out of my hole when — you won't believe this — but someone pushed me back down. I guess the Good Lord had something more for me to do before I left this earth, because one of those guys didn't come back. Right after they passed my hole, another 120 round hit right where they went, and it must have hit one of them directly because he was never found. His last name was King, He went over with us and said then that he wouldn't come back; everyone was always telling him to put his helmet on. Again, Lord, thank you for saving my life.

Like I said before, Korea had a lot of mountains. One day, after I had made gunner, the whole Reg. had to move from one area to another. Let me tell you, we didn't do it at a walk — we were practically running and we were going up this mountain. Here I am, carrying the bipod of the gun and trying to keep up, and by the time we got to the top of the mountain, I just threw the bipod to the ground and said, "Who the hell is leading this outfit? Does he think we are a bunch of pack animals?" With that, someone yelled, "Take 10."

On the evening of Sept. 12, 1951, we were set up on this flat spot near a creek, and we saw a flare go off in the distance. We thought it was the enemy making an attack, and here I am now, the gunner of my section with just 5 rounds of ammo for my 45. Well, that night we stood 50% watch, and the next morning, we found out that we made a counter attack against the enemy. I went down to the creek the next morning to fill my canteen with water, and then went back to my hole to put water purification pills in my canteen. I was standing in my hole just about to put the pills in my canteen when 120 mortar hit nearby. As I dove into my hole, I felt a sting in my leg. I knew right away that I had been hit with shrapnel in my left leg, I also had a little piece that just broke the skin in the middle of my side, and one last piece that laid on my pants at the thigh, that just scorched the material. Like a dummy, I took that piece and threw it away. My leg wound was the worst — it went in one side and came out the other. Four of my section friends carried me back to the Aid Station. We couldn't believe all the wounded that were there. Our Corpsman patched me up before my buddies took me back, so I laid there in the aid station for some time before anyone looked at me. I laid there until after dark and my leg was hurting pretty much, and finally a Corpsman came over to me. He started taping my side and I said, "It's my leg, not my side." After the Corpsman finished taping my side he told me to turn over on my stomach and grab the handles because he had to trim the burned skin from around the wound. Needless to say, it hurt like hell and I gritted my teeth, but that didn't help much.

Like I said before, there were a lot of wounded people and the next morning, they were loading us on anything they could find, including trucks, Jeeps and vehicles that they called Ducks. They drove us to Seoul, where they loaded us on planes and flew us to Puson. When we landed in Puson, they took us to hospital ships, the Repose and the Mennofee. I was put on the Mennofee. My ward had 52 beds on it and before they got me in a bunk, the ward was full. I found out later that our whole outfit was almost wiped out — we had about 750 casualties. They called

The Battle of Bloody Ridge. Along with my outfit, there was the Army's 2nd Cavalry; they had casualties that were on the ship. I also heard that they pulled their outfit back to the States to regroup because of so many casualties. I found out later that one of the guys that I work with now was in the 1st Cav. and he said that the 2nd lost their colors and they couldn't return to the States to regroup, so they went somewhere in Japan to do it.

When the doctor on my ward came to see me, he asked, "Can you bend your foot at the ankle?" You see, when that piece of shrapnel went through my leg, it caused my foot to go almost straight out from my leg. My thinking at the time was that maybe it damaged the muscle in my leg. Of course, when he asked me that I said no, so then he told me to jump up and down on my foot. I almost cursed him out because it hurt to do that. I couldn't even walk on it. The doctor examined my leg and said it hadn't damaged the muscle — "I'm going to put your leg in a cast for 10 days and see if it helps." What the cast did, was force the foot back to its normal position. They really pissed me off because to do this, they gave me a spinal shot to deaden the pain. Wrong! The shot hurt worse than if they had given me nothing. To show you how dumb they were, after the 10 days when they came in to take the cast off, it was chow time. So naturally, it stunk really bad when they cut it off because of the blood that had soaked into the cast from the wound. After they took the cast off, I didn't have any trouble walking. The doctor told me to walk a lot to strengthen the muscle and to go up and down ladders — that's what the Navy calls steps — to stretch the muscles.

In my part of the ward, there were three other guys from the Marines and they all knew how to play Pinochle. After I did my exercises, that's how we spent our days. Every Wed., the Navy had a fire drill, so they turned off all the lights and closed all the shutters on the windows, therefore, making it dark in our ward. Needless to say, we would start yelling to turn the lights back on so we could continue playing cards.

I was doing good with my leg, but there was a guy from the Army who had the same kind of wound as mine. His was a bullet wound and it wasn't doing as well as mine. One day, our doctor says to me, "This ship is going back to Japan to get refurbished. Would you want to go or stay here and transfer over to the other ship, the Repose?" I looked at him and said, "When are we leaving?" When we got to Japan, I was put in the hospital at Yokosuka. The next morning I was eating breakfast, I happened to look up, and who do you suppose I saw? None other than Erv. Hoffman, so I stood up and yelled, "Lucky, you SOB!", and he knew right away it had to be someone from home calling him by that name. He looked around and finally saw me and he raised his hand and I saw that finger bandaged up and he yelled, "I told you they'd pay for calling me back." We both started laughing, just think about it a minute. Who would have thought that two people that used to work together would run into each other that far from home. We bummed around visiting other guys he knew at the hospital and then he had to go back to his outfit. I told him I bet I'd beat him home, and as it turned out I did.

A couple days later, I was awarded the Purple Heart by a Navy Commander, my picture was taken when he pinned it on me. The picture was sent home and put in the paper. You remember I told you that Shirley and I had broken up? Well, you see, she always had these dreams. She called my mother and told her that I had been wounded, before Mom got the Telegram from the Government. From the hospital, I was sent to a rest camp, a place called Otsu, which is close to a larger city, called Kyoto. The Japanese call it the Hollywood of Japan. It is a beautiful city but it was very crowded, so you didn't walk, you kind of shuffled. While I was there, sometime in late Oct. 1951, I got a letter from Mom, telling me that my brother had cancer.

I went to the Red Cross to see if I could get an emergency leave. A couple days later, I was called to the office and told that I got a 30 day leave. As I read my orders, they said I had to report back to Travis Air Base in California and then fly back to Korea to finish my tour of one year. So I said to them, "My brother probably won't get any better, so is there any way that I could stay in the States?" They told me when I got home to get letters from my brother's doctors and also from his minister, stating that they thought he wouldn't get better, and then send them to the Marine Headquarters in Washington, DC. They more than likely would transfer me to some other place in the States.

I flew from Tokyo and landed at Travis Air Base in Oakland, California, on my birthday, which is Nov. the 4th. Some birthday, huh, being in two different countries and continents due to different time zones on the same day as my birthday — that's pretty unique. Flying home, we made two stops before we landed in California. The first place was Wake Island, where one of the battles of WWII was fought. It was in the daytime and looking down at it from the plane, I said to myself, there was no way we're going to land there. It looked like a postage stamp, it was so small. We had lunch there, gassed up and took off for Hawaii. It was dark when we got there and we only had 3 hours before we took off again, so I didn't have time to look around. From there, we headed for Travis Air Base and landed 36 hours later. I forgot to tell you, when we landed in Kobe, going over, we left our Seabees with all of our dress clothes, our blanket and a lot of our other clothes. There wasn't enough room in your haversack to carry all of your clothes. With what I was wearing, I took two sets of skivvies, two pair of socks, my other set of dungarees, my field jacket, toiletries, writing paper, pencil and all of the other gear which I carried in my haversack, plus my M1 and my cartridge belt. So, when I got wounded, I left everything there, and when I got to the hospital in Japan, I didn't have any clothes. They gave me some while in the hospital, and I got more at the rest camp in Otsu, so while I was there, I asked if it was possible to get my Seabag from Kobe. As it turned out, it followed me home; it caught up with me after I got to my next station at Indianapolis.

When I got to California, I got on a train and started home. I had to change trains in Chicago, but to do that, I had to walk from one station to another one. When I finally got home, coming out of the terminal, this fellow walked up to me and asked where I was going. I told him I was going to my home in Walnut Hills. He grabbed my duffel bag and said, "Let's go, I'll take you home." After getting home, I went to see my brother. No one had told him that he had cancer but he was too smart not to know. When I walked in at his home, he looked up and said, "What are you doing home?" I told him they don't need cripples over there so they sent me home.

At the time, I was dating a girl by the name of Hilda Hidden, from the western part of town that I had met before going overseas. One night, I didn't have a date so I told Mom I was going to a basketball game at Walnut Hills High, I saw in the paper that my old High School was playing there. After I had been there for a while, I ran into a friend of mine who was in the Air Force. The ball game wasn't that interesting so we left and headed for Peoples Corner where the Rainbow Club was. After we were there for a while, people started asking me questions about the ribbons I was wearing. I told them that I had just gotten home from Korea and these are the ones I'm allowed to wear. After that, everyone started buying drinks for us, and since I wasn't a big drinker, I proceeded to feel really good. We left there and started across the street to the Anchor Bar, but by the time we got across, we were all the way down at the corner. You see, both places we were at, are in the middle of the block. When we decided to go home, he was driving and we went only about 5 miles an hour. At home, my parents lived on the second floor, and my room was on the third floor. My mom always kept her house real warm, so when I started up the steps, I felt like I was going to be sick. I just made it to the top and got to the toilet and threw up. The next morning, when I got up and went down stairs, Mom said, "You want some tomato juice?" I said, "You must have heard me last night," and she said, "How could I not?" I was sick for three days and right then, I said to myself, it's not worth drinking that much and feeling that bad afterwards, so I didn't too much after that. In fact, I didn't like it that much.

While I was home, I did what they told me about getting transferred to somewhere else in the States. I got a letter from my brother's doctor and also his minister which stated that he was terminally ill and wasn't expected to live very long. I then sent them to Marine Headquarters in Washington D. C. One Sunday, I decided to go to church and ran into Shirley; deep down I knew that I loved her, so I asked her if she was dating anyone. She said no, so I asked her if I could walk her home after church. Dorothy was with her and they both said to come home and have dinner with them. Of course, you all know what kind of people Dorothy and George were — they made me feel right at home. That night, we went to the movies and when we got to her home, we saw that Dorothy and George had gone to bed. She asked me to come in and talk over things, and that's when I got a shock of my life. We were sitting in the living room and she looked at me and said she fell in love with me the first time she saw me. I looked at her and said I guess the feeling is mutual because when I saw you in church this morning, I knew then that I was in love with you. At that time, my leave was almost over and I got a telegram from Washington. It said for me to report to the Naval Ordinance Plant in Indianapolis, Indiana. I realized then that I wasn't going back overseas, so I asked Shirley if she would marry me and she said yes. This was in Dec. of '51, and so we set the date for Nov. '52.

Now, on with where I was going: the address was 21st and Arlington, and it was a Guard Detachment, and this was the place that the bombsights for the Bombers were made during WWII. Since it was run by the government, it was totally fenced in by a tall fence. They had around 6,000 civilians working there — that's the reason for the Guard Detachment. After reading the telegram, I thought to myself, I can go home more often, as I did once I got there.

Once in a while, I would ride the Greyhound Bus. But, most of the time, I would hitch hike; back then people picked you up, especially if you were in uniform. I always got lucky getting picked up. One night, this elderly couple picked me up, and we hadn't gone too far when we had a flat tire. The older gentleman said, "What are we going to do?" and I asked him, "Do you have a jack?" He said yes, so I told him that I'd change the tire; he couldn't believe that I would do that for him. All I said was, "After all, you gave me a ride, so the least I can do is change your tire!"

On the 3rd of Jan. 1952, I reported for duty, and all of the other guys there, were veterans of Korea, just like me. We had a Major for a C.O. and a Sergeant Major who took care of the office. A Sergeant Major has three stripes on top, three stripes on the bottom, and a diamond in the middle, and he's the highest noncom there is. After I got there, he called me into his office and asked me if I had my records. I told him no, because I had come home on an emergency leave from Korea. He asked if I had enlisted, and I said yes, in Nov. 1950, and that I had made PFC. when I graduated from boot camp. I also told him that I got wounded in Sept. 1951, and was at the rest camp in Otsu, Japan, when I got the emergency leave. He said, "I'm making you a Corporal, right now, because when your records get here, they will tell me the same." It wasn't too long after that my records did come in and the Sarge was right: I had made Corporal. Guess what else showed up — my Seabag. So now, I had almost double the amount in uniforms. Not long after that, I took the Sgt. exam and passed, so after only 18 months I was a Sgt. Not bad, huh?

Since the plant was owned by the government, there were a lot of high Navy Personnel stationed along with 35 of us. As a guard detachment, we all carried loaded 45's while on duty. The whole complex was fenced in with a high fence, there was a front gate and a rear one, and a guard was stationed there each morning and evening when the employees come to and from work. While the people were working, the rear gate was closed, only the main would be opened with a guard on it all the time. All employees had stickers on their cars so if someone tried to get in without a sticker, he didn't. When an officer would drive in, the guard had to salute him. All the Naval Officers, along with the Sgt. Major, lived off base. There was also a front walk-in gate that led to the front door where all the offices were, and there was a guard shack there for the guard. He checked everyone's bags. When the people went home at night, they had to pass through gates, so if they had anything in their hands other than an umbrella or personal gear, they needed a pass. You know, there's always a wise guy. I was on one of the gates this night and this guy goes through and holds something up and starts laughing. Fooled you this time! I drew my 45, chambered a shell, and said to him, "If you take one more step, I'll drop you in your tracks." Needless to say he didn't try that again. Another one of our duties was that every two weeks, the people got paid. A bank would come in, drop their guns with us, and cash the checks. The place that they did this was all glassed in and there would be two of us standing guard on each end of this booth. At night, we always had people walking the grounds, checking the gates and all the doors on the building. Every morning and evening, we raised the flag and lowered it. We also had a switch board in our building that we manned on the weekends, holidays and in the evenings. When we got paid, our CO had to go to a bank and get the money, along with two of us with him. We would be armed and do exactly the same as men that drive the Brinks that take money in and out of a bank. There would be one of us in front, and one in back of the CO with our 45's raised in the air.

One day, I was over in the rec building playing pool, which was in the same building as our mess hall. Anyway a fellow, named Jim Egan, came in and asked me if I wanted to go and play some golf. I told him that I hadn't ever played golf; what was so good about chasing a little white ball all over? He said, "Come on, we have a couple sets of clubs here, what do you have to lose, you might like it." So I said OK. As it turned out, I liked it, but a strange thing happened though. I hit a ball over a little rise so I couldn't see where it went. When we got to where the ball was, we found that it had landed in a small creek; next to the ball was a dead fish. Of course, we didn't see the ball hit the fish, but there it was, right next to it.

Speaking about the mess hall, we really had a great cook, and he really fixed some great meals, better than any that I had ever had before in the Corps. Every Sunday, he fixed steak and eggs, whichever way you wanted them. On Fridays, he served these huge frog legs, the size of chicken legs.

So now, every time we go to Houston's for dinner, I always get frog legs. After I made Corporal, there was a Staff Sgt. that had a set of Dress Blues, and he said that they don't fit him anymore, would I like to buy them? "I'll buy them if they fit me," I said, so I tried them on and they did fit. Right after that, I was promoted to Buck Sergeant — that's three stripes, where Staff Sgt. is three up and one down. Dress Blues is a sharp looking Uniform and that's the reason I bought them. The collar was straight and stiff like a priest's, but it fastened in front instead of the back. I think that's where the nicknames Leather Neck and Jar Head came from.

I said earlier, that I was able to get home on most weekends, naturally, I would go see Shirley and we started getting serious and I asked her to marry me and she said yes. We set the date for Nov. 22, 1952. Right after that, orders were sent to every post of the Marines that there was need for people for recruiting duty offices. Since I and another fellow had the most time yet to serve, we were picked. We had to report to Paris Island to go to school to learn the duties of a recruiter. When I got there, we laid around for a couple of months until they had enough people to start the school and other training. While waiting, I met another Sgt. who had just come home from Korea. We introduced ourselves to each other, and he said, "Just call me Ski." Neither of us wanted to be a recruiter, and we both thought, how can we get out of this? As it turned out, it took care of itself because when we got to class, the first thing the Gunnery Sgt. said, was "Those of you that don't have a driver's license can leave." Ski looked at me and I at him, and we both said, "Let's get the hell out of here." A couple of weeks later, we got orders to report to Camp Lejeune, North Carolina. He went to the 8th Marines and I went to the 3rd Bat. 2nd Marines. Camp Lejeune is the home of the 2nd Div.

It seems that every time I go to a new place, it's always late in the evening, so by the time I got a bunk, it was dark in the barracks. The next morning, when I got up, this guy came over and started talking to me in Spanish, and at that time I didn't know there were Puerto Ricans in the Corps. It kind of ticked me off, so I grabbed him by the neck and pushed him against the locker and said, "When you talk to me, you do it in English." I soon found out that there were quite a few of them in the Corps, but after that happened, I didn't have any trouble with them and they all spoke to me in English.

It was July when I reported to Paris Island, and November by the time I got to Lejeune. When I reported to the Weapons Company 3rd Bat., I found out that they were about to leave for the Mediterranean on a cruise. You see every fall, one of the Bats. of the 2nd Div. go to the Mediterranean, for maneuvers. They do this to practice boat landings I guess, I really don't know. Anyway, since I was going to get married Nov. 22nd. and since my brother wasn't going to get over the cancer, I didn't want to leave the States. So I went to the C.O. and told him my problem, and he said, "We will get you transferred over to the 2nd Bat."

Once I got to the Weapons Co. 2nd Bat., I found out that I was very fortunate to have made Sgt. because a lot of the guys there had been in the Corps three years and were still PFCs. Over in Korea, when you got a firing mission, there was a Forward Observer with the Line Companies that sent in firing missions to the guns. It was different here — they put me in charge of the fire direction control center. I had a plotting board that I used, to tell guns where to fire. It took a little while for me to learn but I did, it was easy and a little more accurate. It turned out that I was the senior Sgt. on my floor of the barracks, so I was put in charge. This was a new experience for me to be in charge of people, so I looked at it this way. I have to be tough and not let them walk all over me. I remember, this one time, we were going to have a General Inspection, so this meant we had to have a field day. That means clean the barracks top to bottom, get your gear all in order, spit shine your shoes, making sure that everything is clean. When these guys come, they are wearing white gloves and if they find any dirt or any of your clothes out of place, you were in for trouble with your C.O.

Getting back to the field day, I saw that a couple of the guys were missing and I really got mad. When they finally showed up, I asked them,

"Where the hell you been? You didn't get permission to leave the barracks." They told me that they asked Staff Sgt. Marklen if they could leave and go to the civilian cafeteria and he told them yes, because he wanted them to get something for him. This really made me mad, I didn't know he was standing outside the door when I jumped them. I told them that I was the one in charge here, not him, and with this he walked in and we proceeded getting into an argument about who was in charge. One thing led to another and he finally said, "I'm going to see the old man," and I said, "Go ahead, he'll back me up." Well, he went to see the C.O. and got his butt chewed out. You see, this guy was on the shooting team, and he had already been in the Corps for 6 years and had never been out of the States. Even though he had rank on me, I couldn't respect him, and I never did like him for that reason, and for the way he carried himself, like he was better than anyone else. To me, action speaks for itself.

Another time I had trouble with our Top Sgt. was when our squad bay was outside the office, and we had just come in from field maneuvers. He walked in and grabbed a couple of my men, and I asked him, "Where are you taking my men?" He said, "I got a job for them to do," and I told him, "You're not taking my men, they just came from field maneuvers. Get some of your Remington raiders to do the job." He said the same thing that the other guy said, "I'll see the CO," and I said the same, "Go ahead." He got chewed out the same way. I always did that if I knew I was right. I stuck to my guns, you had to do that if you didn't want to get eaten up.

Our CO was a great guy, because he came up through the ranks and he knew what the NCO's had to put up with. He took a liking to me because of the way I handled myself towards my men and the way I kept myself neat and clean. Because of this, he asked me to be the Company's Guidon Bearer and to be his map man when we were on maneuvers. Let me explain what a Guidon Bearer is and what his duties are. Like I said earlier, when we march, we are three abreast. He is in front of the right hand column, carrying a short flag pole with the Companies Logo Flag on it, holding it in a straight-up position between your arm and side. If you're in a Divisional Parade, you march in front of the Company, right behind the CO. Just back far enough that when you pass the reviewing stand, and salute the Commanding General, you don't hit him with it. What you have to do when you salute with the flag, is snap it straight out in front of you and the CO will say, "Eyes right," and after you pass, he'll say, "front." When that is said, you bring the pole back up and look forward again. When I was his map man, a lot of times just he and I would go out in the boondocks on simulated maneuvers. I would carry the maps. He would plot our position on the map, and the rest of the Company Commanders would call us up on the phone and give us their coordinate on the map. That was my job — to answer the phone and take turns at watch, if we stayed out all night, which we did some of the time. In other words, I was his right hand man.

There was another Sgt. in H and S Company, that lived in Cincinnati, who had his car at the base, his name was Chuck Hyser. There were other guys that lived in Cincy also, so we would chip in for gas and when we got 72 hour passes, we would head for home. Other guys would take turns driving and we drove straight home. Back then, there were no expressways, so we had to take a lot of different roads and go through a lot of towns. If I remember correctly, it took us between 12 and 15 hours to get home. I usually rode in the right seat with a map and to make sure that the driver didn't fall asleep. I remember one night, heading back, we were in a lot of rain, we were still in Ohio on Route 52 heading toward West Virginia. On 52, there are a lot of underpasses and as we approached one, we saw three girls sitting on top of their car, sitting in water. We helped them off of their car and told them we would send them some help when we got to the next town. We had to backtrack a little ways to pick up another route and on the way back, we saw a wrecker coming towards us, so we blinked our lights and slowed down. He saw what we were doing and so he stopped, as we did, and asked us what the problem was, and we told him about the girls and their problem.

It was getting close to the time for Shirley and me to get married and my brother was supposed to be my best man. I got a letter from him stating that he didn't think he could do it, so I asked a friend if he would. His name was Vernon, and I forget his last name. He was a Sgt. also, and he had Dress Blues too. So, he said he would be my best man. I went home a couple of days early and he said he would get there the day before the wedding. Wouldn't you know it, the weather turned bad and he got to the house about two hours before the time. We hurried up and got dressed and my stepfather took us to the church. Shirley was frantic, so they tell me, because I didn't see her until the music started playing, "Here Comes the Bride." Everything turned out all right. All we served at the reception was cake and punch. That afternoon, we took a train to Washington, D.C. for our honeymoon, and our hotel was near all of the interesting places. But, since we got married on the 22nd of November, a lot of the places were closed because of Thanksgiving. We did get into the Washington Monument, the White House, Lincoln Monument and the Capital Building. We took a lot of pictures of everything else. We were there for 6 days and then took the train back home. Now, on the train back, Shirley says to me, "You know, if I didn't know better, I would think I'm pregnant." As it turned out, she was, and nine months and one day later, Steve was born.

While at Lejeune, the first troop helicopter was brought to my attention and also, for the first time, I rode in one. Boy, are they noisy, you couldn't even hear yourself think. We were all sitting around with our packs on, waiting for our turn, and all at once, one of the 'copters coming in for a landing lowered its tail too far and the rotary blade hit the ground, throwing pieces of metal all over. We were lucky no one got hurt. When the 3rd Bat. came back to the States, they landed at Moorehead, which is on the coast not too far from Lejeune. They used the 'copters to bring them back to the base. They put me on one of the high fire towers with a phone and binoculars. I was to call in when I saw the first 'copter coming in from the coast.

One of the things that Lejeune had on base was two golf courses, and they were first class courses to boot. That's all we did on the weekends. They had all kinds of clubs and the balls were real cheap. The Lieutenant that was in charge of the Mortars, was also in charge of the Bat. Golf Team, and after I got pretty good, he asked me to join the team. So, I not only played on the weekends, I also played a lot during the week.

Around June of 1953, they took people that had 6 months or a little more and put us in casual companies. They told us that we were going to be sent to Camp Perry in Ohio, and set it up for the National Rifle Matches that were going to be held in August and September. Then, from there, we were going to the Great Lakes Naval Station in Chicago, Illinois, to muster out. While there, after we got everything set for the matches, all the NCO's were made score keepers and the PFCs and Privates pulled the targets down and marked the spot where the bullet had hit. Before, we went to Camp Perry which is near Port Clinton, Ohio, at the edge of Lake Erie, and I ran into a fellow from New York, by the name of Jerry Frucianti. We started talking and became good friends, but when we got word that we were leaving, his orders got changed. His orders said that he was going to Japan and they were to start a 3rd Div. up. He had to leave right away, so he asked me if I would send all of his civilian clothes home for him and I did.

I hitchhiked home from Camp Perry, the weekend that our first born was supposed to come, but he waited until the next one. I got the call the next weekend that I had become the father of a little boy. Well, I got a box of cigars and passed them out to the guys and headed for home. When I got home, I found out that Shirley had a really rough time delivering Steve, and she looked like she had been through the wringer. The first thing I asked her, was what did we name him, and she said Steven. I said, "How did you spell it?" and she said "Stephen." I said, "No way, I'm going down to the courthouse and changing it to Steven." So, I did! It cost me 50 cents but as I understand now, for some reason or another, they didn't change it. His full name is Steven Kendall, born

Aug. 23, 1952. The other day while talking with Steve, he told me since his birth certificate said Stephen and his passport has Steve, he thought he better get it changed so they both are the same. Since Sept. 11th, the way they check everything these days, it better be the same or you might be in big trouble. So, he proceeded to find out where he had to go, but he got the big run around; finally he found the right place and he had it changed to Steve.

When the rifle matches were over, we went to Great Lakes and while there I pulled MP duty in northern Chicago two or three times. Also, I met another fellow that had his car there, that lived in Fort Wayne, Indiana, so when he went home I would ride with him to Fort Wayne and then hitch hike the rest of the way home. On my way back, we never missed a connection.

When we were discharged, a lot of the guys just got release papers. The government said anyone going into the service after the month of June 1951 had to serve eight years. By this, I mean if you were drafted for two years, you had to serve six years of inactive reserves and the thing applied to those that enlisted for three or four years — is that they had to put the other years left in the inactive reserves.

Since myself and my friend went in before that June, we got our discharge papers. When I was in line getting mine, at the end was another Sgt. He said to me, I will make you a Staff Sgt. if you ship over for more years. I said under my breath, "You can stick that staff you know where." It ended up that we were the only two that got discharge papers, the rest just got released. Bob, that was the friend's name, and I loaded our gear in his car and headed for Fort Wayne. He said, "I'll take you to the bus station and you can go home from there." As we were unloading my gear, this guy walks up to me and asked where I was headed. I told him that we had just got discharged and that I was going home to Cincy. He said to me, "Are you in a hurry?" I said no, and he said that he had to deliver some papers to Cincy and that it would take some time. I told him that's OK, so we loaded my things into the back of the van and headed for

Cincy. After we got to Cincy he said I'll take you to your house, so I told him how to get there and he took me right to my door.

Dorothy and George owned their home, and it had four apartments; they lived in one of the bottom ones. Since they knew when I was getting out, when the upstairs apartment next to their's got empty, they fixed it up a little. The next day George, Shirley and I went shopping for furniture. After Shirley and I got married, I was sending home a $125 dollar allotment every month, so we had over 1,000 dollars saved. I forgot to tell you, that Shirley worked for the telephone company before and after we got married. We had enough money to buy three rooms of furniture and carpet for the living and bedrooms. Of course, Shirley quit work after Steve was born. By the time I got home, Steve was three months old and we took him to the pediatrician. He told us that Steve has a rye neck. By this, he meant the muscles of his neck were not fully developed and to take him to Children's Hospital for physical therapy. I thought to myself, we have a big problem, but Shirley took him to the hospital, and after she came home, she said Steve's problem is minor compared to some of the kids she saw at the hospital.

A funny thing happened between Steve and Dorothy was when he started talking. He couldn't say Dorothy, all he could say was DO-DO. So, Dorothy said, "Steve's initials are SKE, and that's what I'm going to call him," so with this, the whole family started calling him SKE. He was a very good, loving little boy. He and Dorothy and George were very close, and as far as they were concerned, he couldn't do anything wrong. The reason for this, I think, was because when he was a baby, he got colic and if it was during the night, they would take him to bed with them. He had a lot of problems with it until someone told Shirley to change his formula to Wilson Condensed Milk. After she did that, the colic was gone. More on him, later.

We were all still going to Bethlehem Church and I got on the softball team and played first base. We played most of our games down on some fields near Lunken Airport. I remember one game, when I was playing first and the batter hit a ball down towards me, and the pitcher fielded it and threw to me close to the base line. Well, the ball and the runner got to me at the same time; I caught the ball, he hit me and went flying, and hit the deck. I just stood there and held the ball and when he finally got up, he was still groggy.

    I went back to work at Panda, and got a raise to $1.50 an hour. I also entered a government program, where they gave me so much every month. They made up the difference, since by me making $1.50 an hour, that gave me $240 a month. They gave another $120 to make it come to $360. That's the most that you make in a month. When you got a raise, the work place had to inform the government how much it was so they could deduct from what they were sending before down to add up to $360 dollars. To be a tool and die maker, you had to serve a four-year apprenticeship. A little more than four years later, I began making dies on my own, and I must say, I got damn good. We did a lot of work for GE Appliance Park in Louisville, Kentucky, and some of it was really big. One of them that I built, the die shoe was 4 foot square — it was for an electric stove top. The one type of dies that I really liked to build were progressive dies, where you started out with a strip of flat steel or other types of material. It depended on how many stations you had, because every time you brought the punch press together, you changed the shape of the strip. Then, when it came out of the other end, you had a finished part. One year, me and another guy built five refrigerator liner dies — they were only 8 feet square, the shoes I mean.

                                                • • •

Like I said before, we lived in the apartment on Spokane Ave. which was in Walnut Hills; the street was made of mostly old people, so it was a quiet street. One day in 1955, some realtor sold a house on the street to a Black family. There were no other Blacks in our area. It seemed like they lived on one side of Woodburn Ave, and the Whites lived on the other side. I kind of felt sorry for the older people, because they weren't used to living with them in the same neighborhood. Dorothy and George didn't get excited about it at all, but one day, this Black lady came to their door and said she wanted to buy their house. So, they sold it and bought a house on Paxton Ave in Hyde Park, and we also bought a house in Oakley on Mt. Vernon Ave.

We paid $10,000 for it, and it had three rooms on the first floor and two rooms with a bathroom on the second floor, with a full basement. It needed a little work. We had to put new ropes in the windows and some repairs on the plaster of some of the walls. The street was a side street off of Paxton Ave. The lot was narrow but pretty deep, and had three levels in the back — the first one dropped about three feet down from the house. The second dropped another three feet and there was a rock wall about three ft. high around it that gave us about a 10 ft., somewhat flat area, and from there another 25 ft. to the bottom. A fence separated the two backyards. At the time, we didn't own a car, and a couple days after we moved in, I was talking to my backyard neighbor. He said, "I see that you don't have a car, I've got a 1953 Plymouth that runs good that I'll sell to you for $300." I thought about it for a minute, and then said, "OK, I'll buy it." That was my first car. Back then, you really didn't need one because of all the buses. I had it for only a couple of days, when I started smelling gas fumes, so I took it to a station close to the house. He looked at it and told me that the glass carburetor was leaking, but then he said they don't do that kind of work. He told me to go up the street to the Pure Oil Station — they do mechanical work there. As I pulled into the station, I recognized the person inside the building. It was Frank Schirmer, a guy I went to Central with, and had Auto Shop. I said, "Hey Frank, long time no see!" We graduated the same year. Then, I asked him if he owned the station and he said, "Yes, what's your problem?" I told him I had a leaky carburetor; he lifted the hood to look at it and said he can fix it and he did. So, our friendship started all over again. After we started talking, I found out that he used to live near us when Shirley and I lived on Spokane.

After sometime had passed, we started visiting back and forth, and I learned that when I was in high school, and going to the YMCA, I played basketball with Marlin's brother, Emil. After we moved to our house on Mt. Vernon, we started going to Hyde Park United Methodist Church. I found out that the church had a softball team, so I started playing with them. With them, I played first and also caught. One evening, we had to play a double header, plus finish another game that got called because of rain when the score was tied. I had to catch all three games and by the time we finished, I could hardly walk and we still had the old Plymouth, which was a stick shift. I played for a couple years and one Sunday at church, a fellow by the name of Joel Vielhauer, came up to me and asked if I was interested in bowling in the church league. He was in there looking for a couple more teams. By being in the PTA at school, Shirley asked Joel if he was related to the people that owned the Vielhauer Funeral Home. He said that it was his nephew, and Shirley said that she was in the PTA with his wife and that they were good friends. I told Joel that I was interested, and he said that he needed a sub for the next week and would I do it. I told him that I would, we bowled at a place called Condon's on Montgomery Road, in Pleasant Ridge. While there, I noticed a couple guys hanging around and I asked them if they were interested in bowling with me the next year. They both said that they would, so I took their names and phone numbers. I tried to get some people at church, but nobody wanted to bowl. I went to work the next day and asked a guy by the name of Dick Wagner, and I also thought about Frank. They both said they would, so now, I had a team. The next fall we joined the church league and about midway through the season, Jerry (one of the guys that I picked up the year before), was in the groove and on a string of strikes. About the start of the 10th frame, everyone stopped bowling, to watch. I think this made Jerry nervous, because he lifted the next a little too much and it crossed over and hit on the Brooklyn side. He got lucky, because it took them all down and the next two, he put right in the pocket for a perfect game — that was the first 300 game for me to see.

Not long after that, I met Frank's brothers, Joe, Vince, and Cyril, but everyone called him Cy, and another one by the name of Lou. After a few years, the bowling team consisted of me, Frank, Joe, Vince, and John Gallager, who was a friend of the Schirmer brothers. It was really funny, because the four of them were all Catholics, bowling in a Protestant league. Cy was a sub when someone couldn't make it. I remember one year, when we had our banquet at one of the churches, Frank said to me, "Don't tell my mother that I was in a Protestant church." After a while all of the wives got to know each other and so Frank, Marilyn, Joe, Marge, Vince, Mary, Shirley and I started playing cards. We would play at each other's houses, and we played a game called 500. Mary, Vince, Shirley and I bowled in a summer league, a couple of years, until Mary had to quit because she got pregnant with Bill, their youngest.

At about the same time that we got our home, my grandfather and grandmother went into a retirement home, so Dad said to me, "Is there anything here at the house that you want?" Shirley was not into early American furniture, so we didn't take anything. As it stands today, I would have taken the Victrola that I used to wind up and play when I was a kid. Grandma had a brass bed and a beautiful blond secretary that would look good in the house now. I did take Grandpa's ladder and some garden tools.

One of the first jobs I did at the house was put a new roof on it. Since it was two stories, the roof was pretty steep. I took Grandpa's ladder and put a couple brackets on the end, and put it up over the gable. It took me several days to finish the job. When I did, there were a couple of older ladies on the street who came up to me and said, "We're sure glad you're finally finished. We thought that you were going to fall and really hurt yourself." After I finished the roof, I painted the whole house. I had to borrow a 40 ft. extension ladder from my neighbor, because the back of the house was really high. In fact, it was so high, I had to climb almost to the top rung and I still had to stretch out as far as I could reach the top.

In our backyard, and on the side of it, where we walked down to bottom level, there was this huge oak tree that shaded the upper level and I couldn't get grass to grow. It was about 40 ft. square so I got the idea, maybe I could get it blacktopped or put cement over it. I got some bids both ways, and to my surprise, cement was the cheapest, so a week later, they came and did it. I told them that I wanted a smooth job, because I wanted to play shuffleboard on it. They did a super job, and then I thought, how can I fix the rest from the top level, down to the bottom level? So, I borrowed my Uncle Stanley's pickup, so I could get some cement blocks to build a wall across the bottom level. He told me that I had to dig a ditch first and pour a footer, and then lay the block. I already knew that from working with them while they were building houses. Then, I laid the block six high, and then hauled in a lot of dirt to fill it up to the top of the block. I had to put in some steps to get down to the lower level, where I put in some horse shoe pits next to the back fence.

. . .

On Dec. 4, 1956, our second son was born, and we named him Douglas Dean. He was a very active kid. By time he was six months old, we had to take him out of the baby bed because every time I came home from work, I had to put it back together. He used to shake it so hard that it worked the screws loose. Then, after we got him into a twin bed and he got a little older, he started banging his head against the head board. When he started doing this, we thought that it would hurt him, but when we took him to the doctor, he said that it was just his way for him to release. The summer of his 2nd year, I put a fence around the second level, so that he could play there without too much supervision. I was wrong! Shirley was in the house and I was in the basement. I had been in the back doing something, and I needed something from the basement. I don't think I was down there more than five minutes, but when I came back, there was no Doug.

I yelled in at Shirley, "Is Doug with you?" She said no, so I started calling for him and looked down in the backyard. With this, I started to panic and went running out front and looked up and down the street. As I looked up toward Paxton, which was a good distance from our house, I see this man walking with Doug towards me. I ran up to them and he said that Doug was just about to cross the street. He said that he knew

Doug had to live on Mt. Vernon, because he saw Doug come around the corner. After that, we never took our eyes off of him.

Like I said, our house was two levels. Coming down from the second floor, there was three steps, a landing, then you turned left and came down the rest. Well, the Christmas morning after his 4th birthday, after walking down the first three steps, he decides to fly down the rest of the others. I don't know what he was thinking, but he could have killed himself. He was real lucky, because all he had was a large cut on his head. It didn't even knock him out, but when we tried to do something with the cut, he wouldn't hold still. Shirley tried to hold him, while I tried to stop the bleeding by putting ice on the cut, but I finally gave up. Here we are at Xmas, and what do we do? About that time, there was a knock at the door from our neighbor, Goldie, from across the street. She took one look at Doug, and said, "Have you called your doctor?" We told her that we had, but couldn't get an answer. I told her that I was getting ready to take him to the hospital. She said, "Let me call my doctor first." She got an answer and he told her to bring Doug on up to his office. We couldn't believe what happened once we got there, from what we went through with Doug at home. The doctor told us to lay him down on the table, and after we did, he put a towel over the front of Doug. Then, he laid all the things he was going to use, on top of the towel and told Doug not to move, so that he wouldn't knock them off. This is when the surprise came. The doctor put five stitches in his head, without anything to kill the pain. Doug just laid there, very still and didn't make a sound. Shirley looked at me and I at her, and said, "Is this our son he's working on?"

I'm going to jump around again, to when I was growing up. The Cann's used to have a family reunion every summer on my great grandmother's birthday. Between my grandma's and grandpa's families, there would be close to 300 people that came. My Grandpa had it one year, so instead of having it at home, he had it at the school house. They had it until all the older people started passing away, and none of the younger picked it up. So, after we got into our house, I decided that our family should start our own reunion. That was in 1955, and it's still going on yet in 2002.

So now, let's get back to Steve and some of his other problems growing up. I noticed when he started reading, that he would read a little and then go back and start reading the same thing again. Then, when he started playing ball, he would always close his glove before the ball got there. We should have realized that something was wrong, but being young like we were, we let it pass on by. The school didn't pick up on it either. After we bought our second house, in Blue Ash, Steve was in the 5th grade and after the third week he was there, they sent a note home that they wanted to talk to us. We asked him if he was in some kind of trouble and he said not that he knew of. So, the next day, we went to school and was appalled at what we heard. Steve had what you called back then, a tired eye. They gave us the name of an eye doctor to see, so Shirley took him. He gave Steve a lot of different exercises to do. The poor boy couldn't even walk across a flat two by four laying down the four-inch way without falling off of it. One day, Shirley said to me go with him to the next visit and just see what he has been going through. I couldn't believe what I saw — he put these 3D glasses on Steve. Then, he put these two drawings of the same thing down in front of him. He told Steve to bring them together until they were one. Well, when he said that they were together, they were not — they were a good ways apart. I can't tell you how bad I felt after that; here I am, getting after him every time he repeated himself reading and closing his glove before the ball got to it!

I got ahead of the story just now, so let's get back to where we still lived on Mt Vernon. Since I was working a lot of overtime, I couldn't do as much with the kids as I would have liked to have done. That's the trouble you have when you are a tool and die maker. The customer wants his product right now. When Steve started playing baseball, mostly Uncle George and another father coached him. I had to work almost every Sat. so George did all the work. I don't remember how Steve and I got into a club called Indian Guides, but we did. It was a father-son club and we would go to different homes to have our meetings. We did different crafts, like model kits of birds, animals and cars and then paint them. One of the fathers' name was Tom Kinder, and the boys along with Tom and I hit it off pretty good and became good friends. As it turned out, I found out later that Tom was the floor announcer of the U. C. Basketball games and he gave us tickets all the time. This was the time of the big O'S, Oscar Robertson's reign, and back then, tickets were hard to come by. Christmas, one year, Tom asked me to play Santa for the kids in his church, so I did. After we moved, I lost track of him, and one Sunday, when I went to a Bengal football game, and looked down on the field, there was Tom — he was the field announcer for the Bengals.

• • •

Every summer in June, Dorothy and George went to Florida for three weeks, so in 1961, Shirley and the boys drove down with them. Since at the time, I was only getting two weeks' vacation, I flew down the next weekend and then helped drive back home. We stayed at the Penguin Hotel at Miami Beach, which was right across the street from the ocean. I didn't like the ocean that much, and the kids liked the pool a lot more too, so we sat around the pool. One day, I'm sitting there reading a book, and when I looked up, to my surprise, I see Doug dive off into the deep end. As he surfaced, I said to him, "What do you think you are doing?" He looked up at me and said, "I'm swimming," and he was, at the time, 4 years old. Steve had already been swimming by that time; he was going to be 8 in Aug. We did the same thing the next year, and when we're driving home, everyone was asleep except Dorothy and me. She was driving and I was in the seat next to her and happened to look at the speedometer. At the time, we were on a toll highway and back then, they kept the time so if you were speeding, they would know and then give you a ticket. When I saw she was going 85, I said to her, "Are we going to stop anywhere before we get off this toll road?" She said that she wasn't planning to, and I said, "We better, because if we don't, we're going to get a ticket," and with this, she looked down at the speedometer and said, "Oh my God, I guess we better."

The year 1962 was the year that George retired from the courthouse, and they decided that they wanted to build a house in Blue Ash. I said to them, "Why in the hell do you want to move out in the boondocks for? There's nothing out there." After they moved in, and we visited a few times, we kind of took a liking to the town, so one day, I asked George if there were any more lots. He said that there were some over on Elizabeth Place, so we went over and looked at them and decided that we wanted to build. Arcose, was the name of the outfit, that was building the houses, so we all went to their office and talked to them. They wanted just a little more than we could afford in this subdivision, but they had a cheaper model in one, over in Finney Town. So, we went over and looked at it and liked it, but it didn't have a porch on it, like Dorothy's and George's, that has a fruit cellar under it. We asked them if they would build one of them at this site, like the one in Blue Ash. They said since there were three more lots left, they were going to build three houses of that type there. The contractor said for $500 dollars more they would put the porch with the fruit cellar on mine. So, for the total of $18,500 we had our house built and moved into it in July of '63. You see, most of the houses in the subdivision that have porches, don't have the fruit cellar. When I saw how big George's was, that's why I wanted one — it gives you a lot of storage space.

The first year we were there, I painted the walls of the basement with a waterproofing paint. While they were building the house, George would go over every day to make sure they were doing it right. He and I put a mark on the wall, inside the basement, where I wanted to put the water meter. One day, when George went home for lunch, they put the water line in, but they didn't put it where I had put the mark. Believe it or not, they put it into the fruit cellar! Not only that, but instead of running it along the floor, then up the wall on the inside wall of the basement, and then into the house, they ran the line up the outside wall across the bottom of the porch floor into the house, so therefore, that first winter, the pipes froze up. Lucky for me, because I was home and I was able to thaw the pipe before they burst. So then, I bought a heating wire and wrapped it around the pipe, going up the wall and plugged it into the electric plug.

The builders only sodded the front part of the yard and to the back edge of the house, so the yard was mostly clay. I thought to myself: it's going to be hard to get grass to grow. I noticed that one of my neighbors were having sod put on his backyard, so I walked over to the person that was putting it down, and asked him how much it would cost me to do the same. He came over to our yard, and said that it would take 300 rolls of sod, a roll of sod is 6ft. long by 2ft. wide. He gave me a price of 30 cents a roll, which meant $90 dollars for the 300 rolls, and he said he would put them in different places in the back, so I wouldn't have to carry it too far. I asked Charlie Brown, a fellow I worked with, if he would help me put it down, and he said that he would. My luck ran out that day, because it rained quite a lot and by the time Charlie and I got home, it was a mud hole in the backyard. Since it had already been raining before, the guy brought the sod, he couldn't put it around the yard like he said, so we had to carry every roll from one big pile. It seemed like some of the rolls weighed a 100 lbs. or more! Well, we worked at it for some time, and Charlie looked over at me and said that he was so tired, he couldn't do it any longer. By this time, it was getting dark, so I thanked Charlie, and told him to go on home, I stayed at it until I got finished, but when I did, I was so tired, I could hardly move.

Not too long after that, the boys and I drove up to my Grandpa Cann's, to get some trees to plant in our yard. I remembered some of his trees in the woods, where the limbs went straight out from the trunk of the tree. I thought that they would look good in our yard, in a few years, so we dug up three trees. When we got back home, we put one in the middle of the front yard and two in the back. It was Aug. and it was hot and the ground was dry and hard when we planted them.

The ground was so hard, that I had to dig the holes with a pick and shovel. We had to also run water into the hole to soften up the dirt, so that we could plant them. I kind of knew that they were hardwood trees and that they wouldn't clog up my sewer lines. Even though these trees were maple trees, they don't have water roots so they don't go looking for water. Most softwood trees have water roots, and when they go looking for water, they go straight for the sewers. Since our backyard was always wet most of the year, the two we planted in the back didn't last long, and that's the reason I knew that they didn't have water roots. I also found that out this year —

2001 — when we had a little sewer trouble, the drain in the middle of the basement backed up, and we got a little sewage coming up in the basement. I always thought that it was a storm sewer, because when it rained, a lot of clear water used to come up out of it, but then it would drain back out. It happened several times, and it ruined the carpet that I had put down. Coming home from work one night, the water was coming in and while trying to stop it, I thought about trying to use a plunger, and when I did, the water went right out. So, that day that I saw the raw sewage, I called a plumber and I asked him if it was a storm sewer, and he said no, that it was part of the house sewer. He ran an auger through the sewer pipe all the way out to the street and didn't find too many obstructions, so this showed me again that the tree in the front yard didn't cause my sewer to clog up.

The year we moved into our house, was the same year that Charlie Brown and I became good friends. That was the reason I asked him to help me with putting down the sod. The next summer, I helped him put down a cement slab outside his back door. I'll never forget the first time I tried to call him — just look in the phone book once, and just see how many Charlie Brown's there are! I remember that he told me that he lived on a street by the name of Simpson, so when I called the first name, a black guy answered, but the next one was the right one. His wife's name is also Shirley, and we used to visit back and forth. One time, they were over at our house with their four children, and they were all back in Steve's room, watching TV. We were in the living room talking, and I looked toward Steve's room once, and I saw Chris, their youngest, turn the TV off and run towards where we were, laughing his head off; he was 2 years old at the time. There's more about the Browns later.

You remember me telling you earlier about sending my friend's clothes to his sisters in New York, where he was from? I don't remember how we got in contact with each other, but I guess I must have given him Dorothy and George's address, since I was already married. Anyway, that same year of 1963, after we moved in our house, we decided to take a trip to New York, and visit Jerry and Mary Ann. They lived in a community called Scarsdale. Their house was rather large, but it was older, and they didn't have much of a yard. I had heard that property was rather high in New York, so I asked Jerry what the house cost him. He said $3,500. I said to him, "Come down to Cincy, and I'll show you what you can get for that much money." We were there for a week, and he said to me, "I won't take you to the city, but I will take you to the Staten Island Ferry, and you will be able to see a lot of the city." I told him I don't need to see the city because I know what they look like already. They visited us a couple of times and after Marilyn and I were married, we visited them. This time Mary Ann took Marilyn into New York, on the train. They spent most of the day there and Marilyn really enjoyed it.

Since it was July when we moved into our new house, the boys didn't play ball that year. The next year, Steve played C ball and Doug played D ball; back then, they didn't have Tee ball. Tee ball is when they put a baseball on a tee, which is a piece of pipe, mounted on a piece of wood. Then, on the top of the pipe, a piece of rubber tubing is connected to it, that you place the ball on, and then the kid tries to hit it. So, Doug had to hit the ball from another kid that was pitching it to him. I helped both the coaches that the boys had. Steve still had trouble because of his eye problems, but I had to give him credit, because he gave his all and didn't quit. It really surprised me, when Doug did so well; he did have a really good coach those first two years. When he moved up to C ball, he changed teams and there were about 11 kids, and when you saw one, you usually saw them all. They were together all through high school. When the boys got to the junior high, they both played football. Steve played an end; he didn't get to play much, but he stuck with it for the full six years. I do remember, when he was freshman, in one game he caught a ball for a touchdown, and I believe he caught more balls in that same game. I know he always worked hard during practice, but he never did really get a chance to show what he could do. Of course, that's the way Sycamore is — you could be just as good as the other kids, but if you weren't in the in crowd, you didn't get to play much. Doug did play more, but when it came to getting a touchdown, he never got the ball when they were close to the goal line. Let me explain: Doug played both defense and offense; on defense, he played nose tackle and linebacker, and on offense, he played full back. Here's where the rub comes in! When they had the ball between the 20s, they let him run the ball, to pick up yards, but as soon as they got close to the end zone, they never would give him the ball. The thing is, they usually didn't score! The coach knew I was in the stands, along with a lot of other people, because we would yell, "Give the ball to Eppert!" but he never did.

Steve didn't play baseball in high school. I think he thought since he didn't get to play much football, that he didn't want to get disappointed by not playing. Still today, I blame myself for not catching Steve's problems. If I had, I think he would have done better at sports, but like I said before, he never quit, and that's why I've been so proud of him. As I said before, Doug had a good coach the first two years in baseball, so he got better as he continued playing. I remember one year, his coach said to the team, "I need a catcher," so Doug said that he would. I was helping the coach with the team, and when Doug said that, I thought, right then, he's going to get his head knocked off. When he got back there in his first game, he looked like a natural and he became a good hitter along with it. When he got to high school, they didn't have a freshman baseball team, so he went out for the junior varsity, along with another boy by the name of Scott McCall. They both played on the same knothole team, they both were catchers, and both of them were good hitters. Since the team already had a sophomore that was a catcher, Doug didn't think that he had a chance of making the team. He came home one night, after practice, and said that he was going to quit, but I sat him down and told him to stick it out because the coach knew that he was a good hitter. The first game that they played was against Norwood, and they were playing at the old Blue Ash Elementary field. The first two times up to the plate, he hit two balls for home runs, which was over Blue Ash Road onto the railroad tracks.

The summer of '64, Shirley came into the kitchen one morning, and her face and arms were all swollen, so I said, "Let's go see the doctor." After our family doctor had examined her, he said, "You have a heart murmur which was caused by the rheumatic fever she had when she was a kid," and that she had to have a valve replaced in her heart. He told us that there was one doctor in Cincy that could do it, by the name of Helmsworth, whose office was in Holms Hospital. We went to see him, and he said he thought that he would only have to scrape the existing valve, but as it turned out, he did have to replace the old one. After the operation, she laid there for 25 hours in a state of unconsciousness, in a term called fibrillation, which is an irregular heartbeat. The first time I walked into the room, there wasn't much room due to all the equipment that was hooked up to her. The doctor came in while I was there, and I asked him what all they were doing to her and how much more can she take? He said they were finding out — she has had nine different drugs, and been shocked with the spoons 152 times, which will put her into the medical books for all time. We all figured that she might be a vegetable when she does come out it, if she does. Well, to everyone's surprise, the next day, she did awake and she was perfectly fine. She said, even though she looked like she was in a coma, she knew what was going on. The night before, there were three doctors sitting in the room with her waiting for her to come to, and they ate their dinner while sitting there, and she knew what they had to eat. The operation, back then, was different than the way they do it now. They didn't split the chest like they do now. They cut her from the front of the chest from the top to about half way down the front, then around her left arm and then back up the back about halfway. It was quite a long scar. She had to have a nurse around the clock, and I told the doctor that my insurance wouldn't cover that part. He told me not to worry about paying him, just take care of my nurses, so I did. This was in July of 1965. I can't remember just how long she was in the hospital, but it was a few days. When she did come home, she was fine; other than the big scar, everything was normal except, she had to take a blood thinner.

During this time, I missed some work, going back and forth to the hospital, but I had worked 39 hours that week, because I worked a couple of 10-hour days. Well, when I got my check, they only paid me 39 hours straight time, instead of time and half. This made me real mad and I was ready to quit, but I thought better of it, because of Shirley being in the hospital. It took me six more years before I did quit, and that was when I had this big job for GE Louisville. I had three other guys working for me and I was running two milling machines, when one day, the old man's son came down in the shop and started yelling about different things, and no more over time, and I said, "And no more EPP." When I went upstairs and told them that I quit, the old man called me into his office and asked me why I was quitting. I told him that I couldn't work for his son and he said to me, "What if I told you that I was going to take over again?" I said, "That's fine, but when you leave again, it would go back to the way it is now."

Everything was going great and back to normal, until one night in Oct. of 1966, Shirley woke me up and said that she had started bleeding. We worked trying to get it to stop, but didn't have any luck. The doctor told us that if she ever got a cold or anything related, to get on penicillin, right away. Earlier in October, she felt something coming on, so she took some penicillin, right away. In fact, we had a family picture taken at the same time. Getting back to our problem, the next morning I called Doc. Helmsworth, and he said to call the life squad and get her here, to the hospital. While waiting for the life squad, I called Dorothy and George, and they came over. At the time, I had a hot job at work, but I didn't say anything to the doctor about it, but she said to me, "Go on to work and we will go with Shirley to the hospital." That evening, after work, I went to the hospital, thinking that everything was all right, because I didn't get any calls telling me anything different. When I got to her room, her heart was beating so hard it was shaking the bed, so I went looking for the doctor to see what they were doing for her. He told me that everything had cleared up, until a little while ago when this flared up. "We're trying everything to quiet her down, but nothings worked so far." You remember me telling you about her dreams? Well, when she found out about the operation, she was all for it, but when they put her in the ambulance that morning, the doctor said she started screaming and told Dorothy to take care of my boys for me. I guess she knew then that she wasn't coming back home, because that night, about four in the morning, I got a call from the hospital to get there as soon as I could. By the time I got there, she was already gone. It was Friday, Oct. 16, 1966, and the kids stayed with Dorothy and George, because they didn't have school the next day, because the teachers had some kind of meeting. I asked the doctor if he knew what happened, and he said he thought that her heart must have burst, and he said that they were going to perform an autopsy. As it turned out, that's what did happen.

As I'm writing this, I'm crying, because of the fond memories and because I loved her so much, and you know, you never forget your first love. When I got home that morning, and told Dorothy and George, they were devastated because when they left the hospital the day before, everything seemed to be OK. Then, I went into the bedroom where the boys were still asleep, and I woke them. Steve looked me, and said, "What's wrong?" At the time, he was 13 years old, and Doug wasn't quite 10 yet, so how do you tell your boys that their mother is gone? I looked at Steve, and said, "Your mother is in a better place — she's with Our Father the Lord up in Heaven." Bless his heart, I could not believe how he took it! He said, "What do we do now," without that first tear. I said that I had to go to the funeral home to make the arrangements, and he asked me if he could go, and I said sure. I think that he became a grown man, right then. What a kid — I've been proud of him ever since. That evening, at the funeral parlor, with all the people that came, he was the first one to meet them, and he has yet to shed a tear. Every time Dorothy would start crying, she would look up at Steve, and see how he was doing, and she would stop. Even at the church, during the sermon, he didn't cry and I thought to myself, when's he going to break? I couldn't believe it — he didn't at the grave site either, so that night, after we went to bed, I stood at his door waiting. That's when he started, and I went in and grabbed him and told him to let it all out, because it will help you in the long run. We both sat there and cried for a long while and afterward, we both felt better.

Once again, I got ahead of myself! After we got the basement, all painted and squared away, I bought the boys a cheap pool table. When the boys had friends over, they would always go down and shoot pool, so the summer of 1966, I told them that I was going to get them a good one for Christmas. So, after their mother passed away, I kept my word and bought them the pool table.

Dorothy did exactly what Shirley asked her to do, because she stepped right in and took care of me and the boys. Their routine didn't change, because when they came home from school, they would stop at Dorothy's and George's and do their homework. Then, when I got home, she would have dinner for all of us. She basically took care of both houses, and I didn't have to worry about anything. No one asked her to do it, except for Shirley, she just did it. It took me a long time to get over it, and I said then, that I would never marry again. After a while, all my friends would ask me, when are you going to start dating again? All I said to them was that I wasn't ready.

・・・

Feb. of 1968, I was sitting at home, feeling sorry about myself, and it finally hit me, "I am alone," so I went to work the next day, and told the guys that I was ready to start dating again. Here comes Charlie Brown again! He came to me the next day, and said that he had a lady that he would be glad to introduce me to. He said her name is Marilyn Thompson — right now, she lives in Dayton, but I think she would like to meet you. I told him to see if she would come down Friday, so that we could double date, go bowling or something else. Well, she agreed to come down and we did go bowling and I thought, being out of practice for so long, I did OK. After we got through bowling, we went back to Charlie's, where Shirley had fixed a dessert, and we just sat around and talked. I told her about my two boys, and that I had lost my wife in '66. I thought that we had hit it off pretty well, but when I tried to call her the next two nights, she wasn't home. I finally caught her at home a couple of nights later, Marilyn shared an apartment with another lady, by the name of Olive White, and both of them went to the same church, which was Grace Methodist. They also belonged to a young adult group, that met in the evenings at the church. More about them later.

The next Saturday, I went up to Dayton, early, and Marilyn, Olive and I went out and got a bite to eat, and then Marilyn and I went to the movies. While we were going back to her house after the movies, she said that some of the group from church were coming down to Cincy the next Saturday, to a Luau at the Windjammer Hotel. Would I like to go? I told her that I sure would like to go, and as it turned out, most of them were married couples that had belonged to that young adult group. They had asked Marilyn if she would like to join them, since she was originally from Cincy, and most of her family was living there. They called themselves GYA / GSA Alumni, and they met every last Sat. of each month, and every New Year's Day. After Marilyn and I had been there awhile, and I had met everyone, Gene Ritenour, the brother of Max, the fellow that came up with the idea to start the Alumni, said to the rest the group, that Ken's one of us. This made me feel really good about myself, that these people accepted me that fast. I thought, right then, boy, am I lucky here! I've met this beautiful woman, that has friends like these people, and that I better get busy and do something about it.

I introduced Marilyn to the boys, Dorothy and George, and she introduced me to her family. Her mother lived in Norwood with Marilyn's brother, Jim. Her sister, JoAnn, and her two daughters lived in Sharonville, and her brother, Bob, with his wife, Phyllis and his daughter Robin and son, Bobby. Phyllis was pregnant with their second son, and David lived in the western part of town. Her mother asked me to dinner one evening, and she fixed fried chicken, my favorite, with all the trimmings, and for dessert, she had blackberry cobbler, also my favorite. You think she was trying to tell me something? When Marilyn would come to Cincy, she stayed with JoAnn. I remember, one weekend, it started snowing, and I told Marilyn not to come home, but she did, and of course, everyone today knows that she won't drive when it's snowing, even if it's flurries.

I believe it was that Mother's Day, that Marilyn asked the boys and I plus, Dorothy and George to come to her place for dinner. Unknown to any of the rest of us, Steve gave Marilyn a gift, that just floored me. After we were getting serious about each other, the boys and I were coming home from taking her home. Steve was sitting next to me and Doug was in the back seat. I said to them, "Do you have any animosity against Marilyn?" Steve looked at me, and said, "What's good for you, is good for me," and about then, Doug threw his arm over the seat, and said, "One of these days, you are going to get old and be sitting in the house, all alone." Right then, I knew what I was going to do, but first, I had to find out what Dorothy and George had to say. So, after I let the boys off at home, I told them I wanted to talk to Uncle George and DoDo. I went over to their house and told them that I wanted to talk to them about Marilyn. The first thing I said to them was that I was getting very serious about Marilyn, and that I was going to ask her to marry me. "I don't want to hurt your feelings by doing this, because of what you have done for me and the boys." Dorothy looked at me and said, "You know who sent her to us don't you? It was Shirley, and anyway, I am getting tired of keeping two houses!" I went right home, and called Marilyn and proposed to her, and she in turn accepted. The next day, when I went to work, I told Charlie that Marilyn and I were going to get married in June, and when he told Shirley, she looked at him, and said if it didn't work out, she was going to kill him.

We got together and decided on the 29th of June, 1968, and she asked me, how many can I have? All I said was that you get the girls and I'll get the guys. We ended up with six apiece; her sister, JoAnn, was maid of honor, and Steve, my son, was my best man. Doug was in the wedding, also. We got married at Hyde Park Community Methodist Church, and the church was completely full with our families and friends. Most of the group that we belong to now were there, and come this June, it will be 34 years that we have met every month, and every New Year's Day, since we have been married. Being it was in June, the temperature was 98 in the shade, and the church was not air-conditioned. On the way to our honeymoon, which was Penny Rile State Park in Kentucky, we were stopped by the highway patrol. There was not another car on the road and I happened to look up at the mirror, and saw his blinking lights, so I stopped and he gave us a ticket. After we got there, I got an earache and had to see a doctor, and when we got back home, everything got back to normal. Marilyn accepted her role as a wife and a mother, like I knew she would, because of who she is. I thought that she would have a problem from not being a mother before, but as usual, I was wrong, and she and the boys got along just fine. I think the reason for this, was when we were dating, we did some things with them, so they weren't strangers with each other. Oh, there were some bumps in the road along the way, but we all got by them. Still, today, I can't believe how lucky I was when I met Marilyn, and she became my wife. I thank the Lord every day for bringing her to me. I love her more every day, and the last 34 years have been the best years of my life, and I hope they continue for a lot more years. Oh, we've had some moments! I remember one time, not too long after we were married, I got mad about something really stupid, and I said

I'm leaving. I walked out the front door, but instead of leaving, I went over and laid down on the glider and fell asleep. Marilyn didn't know where I went and I don't know how long I was out there, but when I woke up and went back into the house, she asked me, "Where have you been?" I told her that I was out on the porch and fell asleep on the glider. I really think she thought that I had left, I told her that I was sorry and that I loved her and that I won't ever do it again. She did a great job with the boys, and I knew that they respected her, because when they introduced her to any of their friends, they always told them, "This is my mother."

One time, when we were still dating, we had been out and we stopped at the house and decided to sit on the front porch and talk. I was telling Marilyn that my neighbor had this German Shepherd dog that checked the neighborhood every night. She couldn't believe me, at first, but sure enough, while we were sitting there, here he came walking between each house checking things out. Once we got back home, and everything got back to normal, Marilyn and I were talking, and she said that she wanted to have children of her own, even though she considered Steve and Doug her children. When she told me that she wanted to have children, I said to myself, am I doing the right thing, bringing more kids into this world, because of what I knew about drugs going through school, and other things going on throughout the world? But I told her that it was okay by me, but that we would have to add another bed room to the house. The reason for this, was because when Shirley died, we didn't have a will, so the house now belonged to not just me, but also the boys. Another reason was that I didn't want to sell the house, and buy another one, because I liked it here. So, I contacted the contractor that built the house, and he sent a guy out and right away, he said it couldn't be done. I told him what I wanted to do — that I wanted to cut a door in the dining room in the right back wall of the dining room, and make another bed room 11 ft. wide and 18 ft. deep. There would be a little hall between the dining room and the bed room that would go over the steps going down to the basement. This is where the guy said that it wouldn't work, because there wouldn't be enough head room. The next day, while at work, I was telling one of my bosses my problem, and he said that he had just had a room added to his house and they did a good job. So, I got their name. I called them that night and they came to the house. After that first guy said it couldn't be done, I went down to the basement and had a look at what he was talking about. You see, the steps go from the kitchen down toward the outside wall, to a landing, then two more steps to the basement, so I thought to myself, why can't I take the landing out, lower the rest of the steps, put another landing with no steps, therefore, giving me the head room, under the little hall above? When the other contractor came, I asked if my idea would work, so he went down and did some measuring and he said, "No problem." So, I told them I wanted a room 11ft wide by 18ft long, with a closet all the way across the back wall. I also told them that I wanted a door going outside from the room, so they added a walkway from that door, over to the stoop that was outside from the patio door. The room cost us just $3,000, which was not too bad. Around that same time, Marilyn found out that she was pregnant with our first child. Nine months later on Aug. 17, 1969, Scott was born.

That spring of 1969, Evelyn, Bill Morris, Barb, Bill Ross, and Marilyn and I went to General Butler State Park for a weekend. Evelyn was pregnant with Billy, their first, and she was so big, that we thought that she was going to have him there at the park. As it turned out, he was born not too long after that weekend.

I think it was in the summer, not too long after we were married, that the group said that they were going to go camping and canoeing. That's when I found out that Marilyn liked camping. I told her that I had enough of that when I was in the Marines. So, we went, and the two boys went with us, also, and we all enjoyed it; more about camping later.

I remember when Scott was two, we were out in the backyard, and Steve had Scott on his shoulders, running around and Scott was laughing his head off. Speaking of Steve, I think it was when he was a junior that he started dating Linda. Her father was in the brick business and during the summers, he used to work for him at the brick yard. After he graduated from high school, he went to a junior college and took classes to learn mechanical drawing. His second year, he got a Coop job with a company called Bode Finn, and they told him that when he was finished with school, they wouldn't have a job for him. During that same time, he and Linda had already gotten married, but more on that, later. Anyway, Linda's father, John, said to Steve, that he would much rather leave his business to him, than to some stranger. You see, John didn't have a son to leave it to. Steve came to me, and asked what I thought. All I told him was that he would have to go to big companies to get a job in his field, because he didn't have much experience to get hired by a small company. I also told him that he would be a damn fool if he turned down John. So, he took John's offer, and John did the right thing and taught him the whole business.

He even drove one of the big Boom Trucks. Now, as you all know, he is the President of the company.

Now, back to Steve and Linda's marriage, it was the weekend of Labor Day in 1972. At the time, Steve worked at Bode Finn, and they only worked a half day on Fridays. While Marilyn was cleaning his room, she noticed that there was a suitcase on his bed. You see, Linda's parents had a boat on Cumberland Lake, and Steve would go with them on the weekends, but he would take a change of clothes in a paper bag. So, as he was walking up the walk that afternoon, Marilyn asked him if he and Linda were running off and getting married. All he said was, "How did you find out?" She said that she just thought that it was kind of strange, to see a suitcase on his bed. Around that same time, a lot of the group had campers, so on the long weekends, we all went camping. Linda told her parents that she was going with us. A little while later, Linda came, and Marilyn said to them, that they couldn't get married, because they needed to get a blood test. They told her that they did that last weekend. Marilyn tried everything to stop them, but to no avail. It all worked out though — this year will be their 30th anniversary, and they have two great kids and they are now grandparents of a little boy.

After Steve got married and left our home, Doug moved into the new bedroom, until sometime in early '77. The same year, he and Sue got married, which didn't work out, and they were divorced after two years. That same year, I went into that new room and completely did it over. When I decided on doing this, Pete was going to tear down the barn that I used to play in, when I was a kid. I told him that I wanted some of the barn siding for my room. Once he had the barn torn down, I went up and got a lot of the siding and brought it home. Once I got it home, I took it out on the patio and scrubbed the boards real good with a wire brush and Clorox water, so that there wouldn't be any bugs in them to come out into the room, after they were put up. I took all of the dry wall off the walls, then put tar paper in its place, and tore the closet out, that was across the back wall. Then, in the middle of that back wall, I put in a fireplace. At the time, Steve's brick yard sold Pre-way fireplaces. A Pre-way is a self-contained unit, so I put some concrete block down, then put the fire place on top of them, and sawed a hole in the roof to put pipe through. Then, I built a wood frame around the fire place, up to the ceiling, then glued imitation brick over it to make it look like a real brick fireplace. On each side of the fireplace, on the bottom part, I made small closets, and in the upper parts, I put in shelves.

The summer of that year, 1972, is when I quit Panda and had a job, the next day, with Zee Tool and Die. I was to start that next day. When I came home, Marilyn was looking at the paper, and said, "Look at this ad." A place in Newtown was looking for die makers, and since it was closer to home, I went there and talked to the man in charge of hiring. He was so good at his job, that he talked me into coming to work for them, so I called Zee and told them that I changed my mind. The name of the company was Senco. I went to work for them — they made nails, nail guns, staples and staple guns. One of the jobs I did was make three prototype staple guns, to make staples to close up cuts from operations. I worked there a little over two years, and then the building crunch hit, so they had a plant-wide layoff. They said that they didn't want to lay off any die makers, but since it was plant-wide, they had to. Once again, I saw this ad in the paper, that a company on Blue Ash Road, close to the house, wanted a die maker. This time, it was so close to my home, that I walked to work. The name of this place was Saurer Manufactory, where they made battery chargers to charge batteries for cars. I worked there for two years. I don't remember if it was the first year or the next, but it got really cold, I believe it got down to 25 below zero. Going to work that morning, the wind was blowing so hard, I had a hard time walking there. That same year, they told us at work that we had to cut down on the heat in our building.

This was the year that we bought our first camper, which was the little fold down box trailer. Charlie Sellars, a neighbor of ours, came down to help me get everything that I needed to hook it up to the car. I had it sitting in the driveway. After I got everything that I needed, Marilyn asked them to come down for dinner, so after dinner, Charlie and I went out to hook everything up. We got everything hooked up, but the running lights wouldn't light up, so we got to checking, and here, all the light bulbs were missing. Right away, I knew what happened to them, because we had two kids that lived next door to us that were wild, with no supervision at all. One day, I was walking home from work, and here this four year old was beating his mother's car with a hammer. I said to him, "What are you doing?" and he just looked at me like I was crazy.

Like I said, these kids were bad! I had just put a new screen in the patio door. A couple of days later, we went some place and when we got home, the screen was ripped all to pieces. Then, one day, as I was walking home from work, all the kids met me and said, "Wait until you see what's happened now." In the meantime, I had gotten everything that I needed for the trailer, so Charlie was down and was waiting for me in the house. He had seen what had happened outside. As I looked outside, I could see that the chain link fence had been torn apart, and one strand had been unwound. I got really mad, but I waited a little while to cool off, and at the time, their father Don, was cutting the grass. I walked outside and called him, but he just kept cutting his grass, so I yelled, "Don I would like to see you right now." Charlie came out with me, to see what was going to happen — at the time, Charlie was a cop. When Don came over, I said to him, I didn't mind that they took all of the light bulbs off the trailer, but when they destroy private property, that's gone too far. He said to me, "Well, we're going to move;" With this, Charlie left, so I said to him, "When you do move, you better put up a 36ft. fence to hold them in, because when they become teenagers, you won't be able to handle them." The first thing you have to do is teach them right from wrong. It wasn't too much longer when they moved, and everyone was quite relieved.

Earlier that same year, on July 6th, I became a father for the fourth time. Marilyn had our second son, whom we named Todd Kenneth. After he was born, I said to everybody that it seemed kind of weird — I have two sons by two different women. One by each dark complexion and one each light complexion. It's like I was living it all over again, like the first time.

I made a promise to myself that I would do a lot more with these two, even though I did a lot with Steve and Doug. I coached all of them in baseball. Since the older boys played football, I couldn't coach them. When Scott turned six, that was when soccer was started in the Blue Ash area and other areas around us. I took Scott to his first practice and the coach asked if anyone would like to help, so I said I would. It turned out that I liked soccer better than baseball, because every boy or girl gets to play in every game. In fact, one day at work, years later, a fellow asked me, "Why are a lot more kids going out for soccer and not baseball these days?" So I asked him, how many kids did he have on his team and he said he had 14, so I said to him, "How many do you play?" He said that he played nine, and that the other five get to bat. I said to him, that's not playing, just because they get to bat. Then, I told him that I might have 15 to 16 kids on my soccer team, and all of them played at least a half of the game. You see, the kids don't have to be a star to play soccer; all they have to do is play their position and have fun doing it.

Like always, I got ahead of myself again. When Scott was four, I decided that I was going to make bunk beds for each of the boys, so they could have friends stay overnight. We saw in the paper that we could buy unfinished twin beds with drawers under them. So, I sat down and started drawing up a plan on how I was going make the top part. Instead of making it to sit on top of the lower one, I decided to make the top with an opening at one end, and make a chest with drawers in it on the other end. That way, we could put the twin under the opening of the top one. So, Scott and I went over to the lumber yard near us, and ordered all the wood that we needed. A couple of days later, it was delivered and Scott and I went down in the garage and started cutting up the wood for the top half of the two beds. We made the top bed out of 3/4 plywood, along with the cabinet base. As I was putting the base together, I happened to think, I better check the opening of the doors to make sure that it's not too big. As it turned out, it was too big, so I had to cut it down some. I borrowed a router from my stepbrother to do the drawers, and when I got finished with the whole thing, they looked pretty good.

Around that same time, some of the group decided that they were going to start camping on the long weekends in the summer. Of course, we went along with it, so we all decided to buy tents. Wrong idea! The second day it started raining. So, we went to Evelyn and Bill's, and spent the day there. I believe Todd was one and Scott was four. The next year, we all had campers of one kind or another. We had a little box camper that we could pull with the car, while other people had the regular full-size trailers. By this time, the older boys didn't want to camp, so they stayed with Dorothy and George. We first camped at a place in Peoples, Ohio, owned by the Church of the Brethren, then we found out about the Methodist Camp Ground in Germantown, which was closer for us and some of the other people. There is about 200 acres, and it's off in an area away from everything, so we didn't have to worry too much about the kids. There was a swimming pool and tennis courts, but the kids' favorite place to play was an area over the hill, close to where the campers were all parked. We called it the "mud hill," because when it rained, it always got muddy.

All of the group didn't camp, and what happened when we camped, was that one of the couples would take charge and bring all the food, except desserts and steaks. It was always on long holiday weekends that we camped. The people that didn't camp, would always come on the middle day of camping, and bring their steaks. Like I said, earlier, we have a great group because there's no cliques in it; we all get along with each other. It's been 34 years now, and we get together every month and every New Year's Day. The beauty about it, is that most everyone comes every time. Actually, we're like a big family, the kids were like brothers and sisters. One year, we had five boys graduate from high school. Now that we don't camp anymore, when we get together, we either just sit around and talk, or play games. Sometimes, four of us play pinochle if everyone is there. When we were all younger, if someone needed help, a lot would be there to help. We helped paint houses inside and outside, and put new roofing on houses. More later about how we helped each other.

Again, when Scott turned six, soccer was first started in Blue Ash, so we signed him up. When his coach called him to come to practice, I went with him. As the coach was talking to the kids, he asked if any of us fathers would like to help. So, I said that I would, but that I didn't know much about the game. It turned out that I really liked it, and it didn't take long before I kind of knew what I was doing. Scott really liked it too, and in a couple years, he got to be pretty good. I stayed with Scott's teams, because he changed teams every two years. By this, I mean that when he was six, half the team was six and the other half was seven. So, the next year, he stayed with the same coach, but the older boys went with another coach, so therefore, you always had new people that you played with. As I said before, I helped with Scott's teams until Todd started playing, then I started being the head coach of his teams as he progressed.

Both Scott and Todd played baseball, but when they started, it was called T Ball. They called it tee ball, because the ball is put onto a rubber tube, that's fastened onto a wood post, that's fastened to a wooden board, that looks like a home plate. Right about the time that Todd started playing T ball, I had a Pinto Station Wagon, and one evening, I was over at the Dillonvale Shopping Mall. As I was leaving there, I noticed this other Pinto just like mine, but they couldn't get it to run, so I stopped and asked the fellow if he needed help. He asked me if I could take them home, and that he would call a wrecker the next day. I found out their names, because he had his family with him. His name was Dennis Evans, his wife's name was Marlene, and the boys' names were David and Brian. Brian is the same age as Todd, so one day, we were playing this other team in T ball, and you guessed it, there was Brian with his dad, Dennis. He was their coach, and I was helping coach Todd's team. After the game, Denny came over to me and asked, how could he get his team to hit like ours? I told him, that he had his tee placed up too high, causing the kids to pop up. You have to put it even with their swing. Since Brian and Todd were in the same kindergarten class, through PTA, Marilyn and I became good friends with Marlene and Denny. More on our friendship later.

Todd and Brian never played on the same baseball team, but they did play together on the same soccer team. I remember one game, we were having a rough time scoring. Brian was playing fullback for me, because he was good at that position, and he came up to me, and said, "Put me up front and I'll score." I did, and I think he scored. I remember, one night, Brian stayed over and about five in the morning, I heard this noise. I got up to see where it was coming from, and as I passed Todd's bedroom, that's where it was, so, I opened the door. There was Brian, playing in the dark, in the middle of the floor. I said to him, "What are you doing up so early?" He said that he couldn't sleep any longer, so he got up and started playing. I said, "In the dark?"

He said he didn't know where else to play. I think, at the time, he was about six years old. He went camping with us one time, and I was fixing breakfast, so I asked what he wanted. He said that he would like a couple of poached eggs. I told him that I don't do poached eggs, and he said, "My dad does." I said to him that I wasn't his dad, and we both just laughed.

One of Scott's friends, was Danny Estep, who lived down the street from us; they became good friends and still are today. We also became friends with Danny's parents, Dave and Nancy. After we got our camper, when we took our vacations the Sellers, Esteps, and Marilyn, me and the younger boys used to go together. We camped in the state's campgrounds, along with another one of our neighbors, Bob and Pat Winget. I remember, one year, we camped at Cowen Lake. It was right about the time when corn came into season, so we told all of the other neighbors to come up on Saturday afternoon for a corn roast. If you ever want to taste something really good, that's roasted corn. What you do, is get a really big wood fire going, and when you have a lot of hot coals, you soak the corn still in the husks, in water for a little while, then put them on the hot coals, until they are done and boy, does it taste good. Just before we got to the campgrounds, on Friday afternoon, we noticed this farmer had a sign in his yard, "Corn for sale." So, Charlie and I went back Saturday and asked if the corn was fresh picked. He turned around, and walked to the field and picked what we wanted, and came back and said, "Is that fresh enough for you?" I don't remember how much we got, but it was a lot. When everybody got there that afternoon, we had our corn roast and everyone got their fill.

Another time, we went camping at Cowen, the Esteps, Sellars, and us were the only ones that time. Dave had a friend that owned a 30 ft. pontoon boat that we were able to use, but when we got it, we found out that the reverse on the motor didn't work. We decided to go fishing the next morning. After eating breakfast Dave, Charlie and myself set out for the boat. We had to cross the lake to get bait at the bait shop, but when we got out on the lake, the wind was blowing pretty strong towards that side of the lake. As we approached the dock, there were a couple of guys fishing off of the dock, which was against the rules of the park. So, we had just enough room to park the boat on the end of the dock. After we got our bait, I took the helm of the boat. Like I said before, the wind was blowing towards the dock, so as I left the dock, I couldn't turn the boat fast enough. In doing so, I started heading towards the fishing lines of the fishermen. They saw what was going to happen, and started reeling their lines, but didn't do it soon enough, and I cut their lines. They were cussing us out, but all we did was laugh, because we knew that they were in the wrong, in the first place. As we approached the landing, on the other side, there was a father and his two sons standing on the landing. I said before, we didn't have a reverse on the boat, so you had to come in real slow, but I didn't, so I hit the landing pretty hard. When I hit the landing, the father with his sons took off real fast. It's a wonder we didn't get thrown out of the park, and we still laugh about it.

Scott and Todd both took drum lessons when they went into the 5th grade, because they wanted to play in the middle school band. Scott quit after the 8th grade, because all of his friends did. Todd didn't quit, and he was the band's president his senior year. They both played the drums; the homecoming of Todd's junior year, they always had a lot of floats that traveled from the high school over to the football field, which is on Copper Road. Todd came to me, and asked if I would take all of the drummers on the truck, as one of the floats. I told him I would if I could be the first in line, because of all of the stop and go that happens when you are in a line of trucks and cars. I didn't want any of the kids to fall out of the back of the truck and get hurt. The next day, he came home and told me that I would be the first in line. So, we went over to the high school that Friday after dinner, and the kids decorated the truck. As they were doing this, I went over to the Montgomery cop that was sitting there in his car. I asked him if he was going to lead and he said he was, so I told him I was going to be next and that I had a load of kids on the back of the truck. He said to stay behind him about 15ft. and to keep the same pace, and you won't even have to put your foot on the brake. He was right, and the kids didn't miss a beat. After we got to the football field, I went over to the cop and thanked him for doing such a good job. I ended up doing it the next year, and I really enjoyed doing it.

I coached Todd's soccer teams from when he was six years old, until his senior year. I told him that I wanted to watch some of the band's competition. That same year, the band got new uniforms, and they were really sharp. The first competition was at Glenn Este High School; when Marilyn and I got there, the competition had already started. Some of the people were commenting on the kids' uniforms that were on the field at that time. I didn't see Sycamore band at first, because they were over behind the buses. All at once, they started forming up on the left end of the field, and all of the people let out a gasp and said, "Would you look at that school and their uniforms?" As they were playing in front of us, I saw Todd drop one of his drum sticks, but he kept on like nothing happened, and the guy that was grading them, reached down and picked it up and handed it back to Todd, and did not mark anything down against him. Later in the fall, the band went to Columbus, Ohio, to compete in the state competitions. It was the time that Bowling Green, where Scott was in college, had their parents' weekend. Todd's band competition wasn't until late that night, so we were able to get there just in time to see them perform; they made top scores, like they did at all of their competitions.

When Scott and Todd both became old enough to join the Cub Scouts, they did. I don't remember if it was in the spring or fall that they had a lad-dad weekend at Camp Freelander. Fathers and sons would go there and stay in small tents. We would do different things with our son — play games, do crafts. I remember, one year that Todd and I went, as we were walking back to our tent with the others, a big, black cloud formed overhead. Jack Hern said to his son, Jimmy, that they were going home because he didn't want to get all wet. You see, we all knew that these little tents that we were in wouldn't keep us dry. A couple of the others left too, but Todd and I stayed until it started blowing really hard. I said to Todd, "Let's get out of here before it gets worse," and by the time we got to the car, it was really blowing and also raining hard. After we got on the road, there were a lot of tree limbs and other stuff all over the road. We found out later, that we were glad that we left, because the ones that stayed, got soaked and had a rough night getting any sleep. Most of the other times, Scott, Todd and I had a lot of fun. Scott didn't want to go into the Boy Scouts, but Todd did.

In 1984, Todd's troop went up to Wright Patterson, at a Scout's jamboree, where a lot of Boy Scout Troops get together and do a lot of different activities and play games. The troop next to them was from Canada, and as they were talking back and forth, they asked our boys if they would like to come up to their camp in Haliburton, Canada. It's about 150 miles north of Toronto. After they got home that year, the Scout Master and a couple of the fathers got to talking about it, with the kids and they all thought that it was a good idea. Todd came home and told me about it, so I went up to the next meeting and told them that I was interested in going. I told them that I had a truck and that I could pull their utility trailer that hauls all the gear. They told me that would be great, so the kids had a car wash, and the mothers had a cookie sale to make money for the trip. We ended up with 29 people going, so we rented two 15-passenger vans. We packed the food that would spoil in dry ice, and other foods in the truck first, and then put most of the other gear on top of it. We also put some of the sleeping bags in the back of the truck. The Scout Master got everyone a red tee-shirt with our troop number on them, and a red baseball cap, so that we wouldn't lose anyone. Everyone packed a lunch for when we stopped, so we took off early one Saturday morning in Aug. 1985, and headed for our first stop, which was Niagara Falls.

We got there at about six that afternoon, and ate at McDonald's. From there, we went across the border into Canada, and slept in the oldest church in Canada. The next morning, we started north. On our way, we went through a lot of small towns and going through Toronto, which is one of the larger cities in Canada, we found out that it was very clean city. After we left Niagara, we traveled along Lake Ontario, and saw some beautiful scenery, all the way to Toronto, then we headed north again. Halliburton is about 150 miles north of Toronto, and when we got there, we were met at a staging area, where they had pontoon boats. They took all of us and our equipment to our area where we going to stay — you see, where we were, it was mostly water. After we unloaded our gear, we got back on the pontoon boats and were taken to another place, where we picked up our transportation for the week. Most of us got canoes, and I think we also took a couple of row boats. They also gave us a box that had a hole in it to use for a toilet.

They told us to be careful when we sat down, because some varmint might be in there. The water was so pure, that all we had to do was put a 1/4 teaspoon of Clorox in five gallons of water and then we could drink it without getting sick. One day, everyone went scuba diving, except a guy by the name of Steve and myself. There was a lake near us called Hidden Lake, so Steve and I decided to check it out. We got in a canoe and paddled for about 3/4's of an hour, pulled into shore, and then walked another 3/4's of an hour until we got to this lake. When we got there, there was only one canoe with just one paddle, so we got in and Steve started paddling and I started fishing. I was using artificial bait, and as I threw out my line right away a small mouth bass grabbed the bait and took off. Since it was my first time fishing in this manner, I really didn't know what to do. Steve told me, try not to let him go under the canoe, because you will probably lose him. So I was careful not to let him go under the canoe, and as I got him to the canoe, Steve grabbed him with our net. It was about 18 in. long. They told us when we got there, that we couldn't keep anything under 12 in. A little while later, I hooked another one, about the same length, only this time, as Steve was about to get him in the net, he wiggled off the hook. After that, we didn't have any more luck, and it was getting late, so we walked back to our own canoe and went back to our camp. It turned out that I caught the largest fish. We decided to put all of the fish that were caught that week on the dry ice that we brought, until Friday to eat. That way, for those that wanted fish for supper that night, there would be enough for everyone. That trip turned out to be a lot of fun for everyone, and as it turned out, it only cost everyone $100 each.

After we got back from that trip, that fall of 1985, Scott came to me and said he and some of his friends were going to get in an indoor soccer league, and wanted to know if I would be their coach. At first, I said no, because I didn't know anything about indoor soccer, but then I said I would. Like I said, I didn't know what we were getting into, but we found out that first game. It's played somewhat like hockey, with almost the same rules. What the other team did, was hit the side board of the field with the ball, then pick it up on the other side of our player and take off with the ball, towards our goal. We all learned from that first game, and by the end of that first season, we started getting pretty good. I coached them for only two years, because the team kind of broke up. Scott played for another team in 1987, his senior year, but he ended up breaking his leg. At that time, we didn't know it, but Scott was anemic and he had a hard time getting the leg to heal. They took the cast off too soon, and when they put it back in a cast, they didn't do it right. and today, he kind of walks a little on the side of his foot. When he gets older, it will probably give him some trouble.

On March 8, 1986, Doug married Terry Yearion, and as you know, they have 3 children. Ben is 10, born on Oct. 5, 1992, Katie is seven, born on Aug. 24, 1995, and Andrea is three, born on Mar. 18, 1999. They are very good kids, and both Ben and Katie are good readers and are good students. Ben is playing basketball, and has joined the Cub Scouts; Katie has been taking dance classes for the last couple years and really likes it.

Towards the beginning of fall in 1986, Marilyn came to me, and said, since we had been married, she hadn't asked for too much. She said that she wanted to do some things to the kitchen, so I thought about that for a little bit, and said to her "How about getting you back in the family again?" You see, when the older boys left, you all know what I did to that room that we had. When the boys and I were in there, she was in the kitchen and didn't know what we were doing or what we were talking about. So, I told her that I going to do something about making the room larger. I guess I said something to the group about that, because Warren Snodgrass came up to me and said, "Let me look at it." Like I said before, the kitchen was in the middle of the house, and in the middle of that, we had an 8ft. patio door, so I thought that if we had the new addition put to the end of those doors, it would work out. Well, when Warren came down, he said to us that he could cut the brick and then we could extend the kitchen, out into the addition. So, we agreed to let him do the addition, and his one son helped him. He told me to get the foundation put in and get all of the material, and he and his son would come down and build the addition. He told me what all to get, so I went to Steve, and told him what I needed. Since he was in the building business, he probably knew where I could get what we needed. He told me where to go, so I did, and got everything that we needed. The first part of October, they got started. I couldn't believe how fast they put it up, when they had the outside walls up and were putting up the struts for supporting the roof. Warren said that he didn't think that we would lose the ceiling of the first addition. As it turned out, we didn't, because he was able to tie the struts in with the other ceiling.

Since we put in a bay window in the back, we can sit down at our table and watch the damn squirrels eating our apples, while we eat our meals. At the same time that we did the addition, we put in new kitchen cabinets all throughout the kitchen and we did extend them into the new room. We had the door going outside moved farther out, so we could put in more cabinets. Then, on the other side of the door, we had a lot of room, so I decided to put in a long cabinet for storage. On top of that, on each end, I put up book cases and in the middle, I made a two-shelf cabinet with glass doors, so Marilyn could put some of her Precious Moments Pieces on display.

Scott graduated from high school in 1987, and decided to go to Bowling Green University, not knowing that he didn't have enough credits, since his school counselor said that he was all right, so he had to go to summer school. As it turned out, that's when he met Kim, who was from Blissfield, Michigan. One of the girls that graduated with Scott went to Bowling Green too, and introduced them to each other. She used to come down and stay with us sometimes on weekends, and the first time, I told her that she could stay with us any time that she wanted to. Scott's first two jobs were in Michigan, so he lived in Kalamazoo in an apartment. Then on June 19, 1993, he and Kim got married.

Todd graduated in 1990, and decided that he wanted to go to Ohio State. He wanted to be a mechanical engineer, but it didn't work out, so he became an industrial system engineer. He graduated in 1995, the summer before he got a job at Ilsco, where I was working. The way that happened, was that same year we got a new boss, by the name of Dave Flynn. He wanted to make some changes and he came back to the tool room a lot to talk to us. The first time I met him, I kind of liked him, because he was that kind of a person that anyone would like. One day, I asked him if he needed any help, and he asked me why, so I told him that Todd, my son, was going to be a senior next year, and his degree was in industrial system engineering. He looked at me, and said that he would like to talk to him, so Todd went and talked to him and got hired. During that summer, I found out just what kind of a son I had, by the way he handled the people that worked under him. It's funny, the way things worked out, because Dave and I became good friends, not because of his hiring Todd, but because something just clicked between us. Todd and Dave have become best of friends, also, and Dave is Todd's mentor, so to speak. They respect each other. Not too long ago, at one of Scott's gigs, but, let me explain what a gig is. You see, Scott, and three other guys — Dave Evans, Mike and Mark Maley — started up a band, and this year, they started playing at the Fire House Grill. One night, Dave came to one of them and I thanked him for what he had done for Todd. What he said to me made me feel real good: he looked at me and said to me, that right now, he's ahead of me as far up the ladder.

That same year of 1990, the year that Todd graduated from high school, we put a new roof on our house. A lot of the group came down, took the old roof off, put tar paper on, then a new roof over it. We got done just before it started raining. I'm talking about women and men both nailing down shingles. Most of them over 50 years old or older.

I'll never forget our experiences years, later in 1993. As you all know, on our 25th anniversary, Steve gave us the cruise to Alaska. Marilyn said we should make him an album. In doing so, we were going through some pictures. Karin and Todd happened to be here, and all at once, Karin started yelling "Todd, this is you!" Well, we didn't know what she was talking about until she showed us. Here it was, a picture of me when I was in the service that looked almost like him. Right then, I said I was going to put it into my wallet for a keepsake.

. . .

I'm back, it's been awhile for me to get back on the computer, so here goes. I said before, that I would get back with Marlene and Denny. We did a lot together as friends, and this is where our 25th anniversary cruise came about. Steve knew about our friendship, so he asked Denny, what does Dad talk about where he would like to go sometime? He told him, that he always would like to go to Alaska someday. A couple of weeks later, Steve and Linda asked us to out to dinner with them. As we were finishing, Steve pulls out this large envelope and hands it to me and says to me, "Open it." As I did, I pulled out this magazine with a picture of Alaska on it. I looked at him and said, "Is this what I think it might be?" He said, "Yes, it's a seven day cruise and seven day trip through Alaska." What a surprise! As it turned out, we were not alone. Marlene, Denny, Jo Ann and Ron decided to go, also.

We left Cincy on September 2nd, 1993, flew to Seattle, and then got a bus, which took us to Vancouver, Canada. When we got to border between the U.S. and Canada, the bus driver stopped, and asked if anyone was going to do anything other than going home or on a cruise. No one said anything, so when the customs person got on the bus, the person in front us said that he was going fishing! We thought that we were going to be delayed, but thankfully we weren't. We took an extra day on our trip, so we could see some of Vancouver, so we took another sightseeing bus that took us to different places. The first place was an old Native American camp, where there were a lot of totem poles. I forgot to tell you, that the driver told us that every stop that he took, he would give us 20 minutes to get back on the bus. There were two women that did not do that the first time we stopped, so the driver said the next time he stopped, if everyone was not on the bus in time, he was going to leave, so after that, they were the first ones on the bus. One of the stops was at these beautiful Botanical Gardens, I mean there were a lot of them, flowers all over the place. We stopped some more places, but I can't remember them all. Then, we went back to our hotel to get our luggage — you would not believe how much we had — put it on another bus that took us to the cruise ship, which was the love boat from the Princess Line. It was the same boat that was on T.V. The real name of the boat was Star Princess. We boarded on Saturday, September 4th, 1993.

• • •

Here is what our itinerary looked like: Vancouver to Seward 9/11/93, seven nights on board ship.

> Sat. — Sail from Vancouver, Bon Voyage
> Sun. — Cruising through the inside passage
> Mon. — Ketchikan, Salmon capital of the world
> Tues. — Juneau, Alaska's Capital City
> Wed. — Skagway, built in the Klondike Gold Rush of '98.
> Thur. — Cruising though Glacier Bay National Park
> Fri. — Cruising College Fjord
> Sat. — Seward

When we got on board, we were told that we had gotten upgraded from a lower deck to the deck next to the top deck. That is, from a small room, to a much larger room. We left port between five or six o'clock, so we decided to go eat, since we had the first seating, which started at 6:30 pm. Let me explain, since there were over 1,500 or so people aboard ship, there are two seatings at each meal, and we had the first seating; the second seating started at 8:30. The dining room was on the Fountain Court Promenade Deck 7 Aft.

Here I go again, getting ahead of myself! When we got on board, we found that we had gotten upgraded from a lower deck to higher deck, like deck 3 to deck 13, which is one deck from the top deck, which is deck 14. So, we asked them how come, and they said, because we got our money to them early. So, we went from a small room, to a really nice room. From bunk beds, to a full-size bed, and a room about the size of our office. So, if any of you ever decide to take a cruise, be sure you get your money in early.

Decks six, seven, and eight, were where most everything that you wanted do was — that's where the shops were, also that's where the shows were every night. The shows were on 7th deck; the first night featured a comedian, by the name of Jay Hoyle, and he was really funny. They put on a good show every night.

The rest of Saturday, we walked all over the boat, checking where everything was. We found out that you ate about anywhere you wanted to. Believe me, it took most of the day. The next day, as we cruised through the inside passage, you would not believe the scenery along the shoreline. We even saw a bear off in the distance. Everywhere we went, you could not put your camera down, you had to take a picture, because everywhere you went, the scenery was so beautiful. That night was dress formal, so we all went back to our cabins and got dressed up for dinner. All us guys put on our tuxes and women put on their gowns, so we all looked very sharp as we went to dinner.

• • •

I don't know why, but I got up early the next morning, and went up on deck 14, and saw that we were about to dock at the harbor of the town of Ketchikan. We ate, then walked into town, which wasn't too far. If I remember right, we all went in different directions for some reason or another. Marilyn and I just started walking and came to this bridge, and looked down into the water and saw all these large salmon. The town was like some of our country towns here — small, but everything here that you needed. One thing you didn't see was too many cars. I forgot to tell you, that you had to get back on board by 5:30, because they were leaving by 6:00. More about Ketchikan: in itself, it is considered one of the most livable cities in the United States. It has a gentle climate and lush natural beauty. We got lucky the day we were there, because it is called the Rain Capital of North America, but we had a beautiful sunny day. It is known as the first city of Alaska. It is the first town along the Inside Passage, located on Revillagigedo Island.

Originally, Ketchikan was a Tlingit Indian camp, but in the late 1800s American pioneers arrived, and began to exploit the salmon fisheries. In the early 1900s, it grew, as a result of the Gold Rush. When the train stopped at the summit of White Pass at the Continental Divide, they unhooked the engine and took it around to the back of the train and hooked it again. The gold and copper mines closed down during World War I, and salmon fishing and lumber, again, took over as the town's major industries. The day, 9/7/93, when we got up, we were in Juneau, the capital city of Alaska. It was named after one Joe Juneau, a gold prospector, who found nuggets as big as pears or beans, in the area, in 1880. During this time, three of the largest gold mining operations in the world were located in Juneau. Over $158 million in gold was removed by these mines, between 1880 and 1944. It's the largest city in the United States, with over 3,108 square miles. The area partly comprises of rain forest, lakes, mountains and ice fields. While we were there, we got on a bus and drove through a lot of old, winding narrow streets, up in the hills for a salmon bake for lunch. It was raining, but the place was covered with plastic, so we didn't get too wet. While we were there, Ron panned for gold. Then, I think we went back somewhere and got another bus, which took us to Mendenhall Glacier. When we got there, it was raining, and kind of foggy, so you could not see a lot. At some distance, I did see eagles sitting on the bank of the river. On the way back to the ship, we did get to see some mountain sheep up on the mountains. It's funny — you would think with Alaska as big as it is, that you would see a lot of animals, but we didn't.

The next day, 9/8/93, we got off at the town, called Skagway. After the ship docked, we got off and hopped aboard White Pass Railroad Train, that traveled over 100 miles of track, then went up this long hill, which we had to flip our seats, so we were facing front again. During the gold rush days, its inhabitants numbered over 10,000, but now, there is only about 800. There wasn't a lot to see, because it is surrounded by mountains, and the town wasn't that big.

I don't remember what day it was, but Denny, Marlene, Marilyn and I were in where they put the shows on, and everyone there was learning to line dance, so we joined them. Marilyn and I tried, but we gave up after a little while. Not too long after that, when we got back together again, Denny says to me, "We're going to be in the show Friday night." About that time, here comes one of the cruise people, and hands me this recording of 9 to 5 music, and says, "You're going to be Dolly Parton in the show, and Denny is going to be Michael Jackson doing, 'I'm, Bad, I'm Bad.'" I'll get to that later.

Thursday, Sept. 9th, 1993, we cruised through Glacier Bay National Monument, which is widely considered to be the most spectacular fjord complex in the world, and certainly the most famous. The Bay is the largest monument in the U.S., containing 13 active tidewater glaciers and 10 glaciers, which extend more than 10 miles in length. 200 years ago, the Bay did not exist — the entire area was covered by a single ice field, which extended into Icy Strait. Since that time, the ice has retreated, carving out the Bay, and leaving behind the magnificent scenery. All of us went up on deck to have a look at what was going on. When we got there, we kept hearing this noise, like the sound of a rifle being shot. It was the glacier calving icebergs. While up there, we did get to see some seals lying on some ice particles floating on the water, and another cruise ship coming the other way.

On Friday, Sept. 10th, 1993, we cruised through an area, that's called College Fjord, where there are a lot of glaciers with the names of different colleges. That night after dinner, like I said before, Denny and I were going to be in that night's show. Before the show, the M.C. called us up to the stage, and introduced us to the audience. Then, we went backstage to get dressed, Denny went first and did a good Michael Jackson. A couple of others did well, also, and then, here I come, all dressed up as Dolly, with these large breasts. Every time I would move, there was a hose connected to my breasts that would make them larger, so I got a good laugh out of it. Throughout the next day, on our way to Seward, everyone that passed me would say, "Hi, Dolly." How about that! I'm a Star.

Saturday, Sept. 11th, 1993, we docked at the Seward Pier, and from there, we traveled on a motor coach, along the Seward and Sterling Highways, en route to Copper Landing and Kenai Princess Lodge. We stayed there for 2 nights. The place was really nice, and we had our own housing, each with a two-room bungalow. We all went on our own way part of the time. Ron, I think, went panning for gold again, Jo and he did something else too, I think. Marilyn and I walked around and checked out some of scenery. There were a lot of tours, but we didn't do any of them, because they cost too much.

On Sept. 13th, 1993, we motor-coached from Keni Princess Lodge, to the city of Anchorage. Leaving Copper Landing, we traveled along the Sterling and Seward Highways, to Portage, at the end of Turnagain Arm.

From there, we traveled to the shores of Cook Inlet, and to the city of Anchorage, which took 3 and 1/2 hours. This was the only place that we were on our own. We were told that we were going to stay in a hotel there that night, and to pack an overnight bag for the trip on the train to Denali, the next day. They took us to the hotel and we got to our rooms. When we got there, they told us to leave our other bags out in front of our doors the next morning, and they would take them to Fairbanks, for the delivery to our hotel room for tomorrow evening. After we got our rooms, we left the hotel to find a place to get something to eat. We found a hamburger place, and after eating, we began walking; Denny, Marlene, Marilyn and I went one way and Jo and Ron went another way. The four of us were walking, and the girls saw this shop and went in. Denny and I waited outside, when three Alaskan Natives walked towards us, two women and one guy. They stopped, and started talking to us. We couldn't understand them, but as they were talking, the guy started laughing, and I said to Denny, that the girls were trying to proposition him, and started laughing.

The next morning, we were taken from the hotel, to the rail depot with our small carry-on bags that we placed under our seats on the train. These were unusual train cars — they were double-decked cars, and the top deck was all glass, so you could see all over; the bottom deck was for dining. We ate breakfast soon after we departed for Denali National Park, which was about 7 and 1/4 hours away. We spent the night there. The next morning, we boarded a school bus for a Natural History Tour; the diversity of the landscape became clear, as we traveled from a Taiga forest, to the vista, afforded by the sweeping tundra. The views of the Alaska Range were spectacular! From there, we visited the sled dog kennels and park headquarters; that took about 3 hours.

Then, we got back on the Ultra Dome Train, heading to Fairbanks on the same car that we were before. We went back up on the top part, and just relaxed and again, viewed the changing landscape. It didn't matter where we went because the scenery was beautiful. I'm not a camera buff, but I couldn't put my camera down! Every place we went was more beautiful than the last one. The trip lasted about 4 and 1/2 hours. From the Fairbanks Depot, we went to Fairbanks Princess Hotel. By the time we got there, it was beginning to get dark, so we walked around and found a place to eat and then went back to the hotel to sleep. Our suitcases were there when we got back.

The next day, Sept. 16th, 1993, we boarded a riverboat for a cruise, to join he Brinkley family, operating an authentic Sternwheeler traveling on the Chena and Tanana Rivers. On the way, we stopped at an 'Old Chena Village' where Native guides shared a glimpse into the history and culture of the Athabascan Tribe. On the boat was a young lady, dressed like an Eskimo.

Since there's not many roads in Alaska, the way they got around was by airplane, and while on the boat, they showed how little space they needed to land or takeoff on, which was not much. The boat also stopped at an area offshore, where a woman had a team of Husky dogs hooked up to a sled and showed how they pulled it.

That afternoon, we went sightseeing in Fairbanks, which calls itself Home to the northernmost institution of higher learning, the University of Alaska. They had a museum that is renowned for its display of Native American and Eskimo Arts and Crafts. We were also able to visit a segment of the Trans-Alaska Pipeline. Let me make a comment right now: if anyone gets to read the letter of mine and decides to go on a cruise, take the Alaska one, along with time on land like we did, because you won't believe the beauty of Alaska. From there, we flew back to Seattle, where Marilyn, me, Jo and Ron were met by Terry, Jo's daughter. Marlene and Denny took another plane home. We went with Terry to her house, and stayed with them for a few days before returning home. While there, Ron and I helped Rory build a deck, off the back of their house. We also took a trip to Mount Rainier National Park, to look at the devastation caused by the eruption of the volcano atop of Mount Rainier. Boy, what devastation! Everything was gone, no trees, no grass, nothing left but dirt and gravel.

• • •

Todd graduated from Ohio State in 1995, and went to work for Ilsco. He was still dating Karin, and Marilyn kept asking, "When are you going to ask her to marry you?" He kept telling her to quit pushing him, and that he would get around to it, when it was the right time. They got married on Nov. 22, 1997. Remember, awhile back in my story, when we were going through some pictures, Karin asked about the picture of me that looked like Todd. Well, guess what? They got married on the same date that Shirley and I got married Nov 22, 1952, 45 years earlier.

I retired from Ilsco the last day of Feb. 1997. I was going to do it in 1996, when I turned 65, but one of the guys that worked with me, said to me, "Why don't you wait until next year, and go out with me?" So, I did. Ilsco threw us a retirement party, and our families were invited, which was very nice. After the party, the boys, Marilyn and I were sitting around and talking and one of the boys said, "Hey, Dad, why don't you try to get a job at the golf course?" So, I said, "I think I will." So, the next day, I went to the golf course to see about getting a job. As I walked into the clubhouse, I ran into a guy, by the name of Fred Reuacher, that worked there. Our boys played football together in high school, that is Steve and Doug, and we got know each other, going to games. Fred was working that day, and he said, "What are you doing here?" I told him I was looking for a job, so Fred said to Bill the boss, "Hire him because he's a good guy," so Bill hired me. More later on this subject.

After the party, the boys said to me, come out to our cars, we have something for you. We went to the cars and they hand me a big box; in it was a set of golf clubs. Scott and Todd said they were off the rest of the day, so let's go play a round of golf. We went out to Kings Island golf course, the small short one. I used my new clubs and liked them. After playing seven holes, Todd and Scott had me down by a stroke. The next hole, I had a good drive, and both boys didn't. The next shot, I put the ball about three feet from the hole, for a birdie. I ended beating them, with my new clubs. How about that?

Since working those two months in 1967, after turning 65 in 1966, I was afraid of messing up the amount of my Social Security checks. You see, you're only allowed to make so much a year, and if you go over that amount, they penalize you. I worked a lot of overtime, those two months, so I went and told Bill that I had to wait until the following year to start and he said that it would be okay. So, when I did go back, I asked if Fred was around and got a real shock; they said, he came in one day, and said he had cancer and took a cart and drove around the course one last time. He died not too long after that. As I'm writing this part, it's Mar. 26, 2014, and I'll be starting my 18th year working at the golf course.

The year 1998 was a bad year for us. Marilyn found out that she had breast cancer, and so she had a lot of chemo and radiation. She kept working during this time, but it made her very tired. After all the chemo and radiation, she started feeling better, and every year, she would go see her doctor to see if everything was all right, and she always got good news that everything was all right. More later.

As most of you know, we did a lot of traveling to different places with Marlene, Denny, Jo, and Ron. Other than Alaska, I can't remember all of them, but I know we went San Francisco with Marlene and Denny and, while we were walking around, Marilyn said that she had lost part of one of her capped teeth, so we went back to the hotel. I believe it was on a Sunday. I got the phone, and found a dentist at his office. We told him that we had just got into town, and told him what had happened. He asked us where we staying, and we told him, and he said that he was right around the corner from us, and to get there within the next hour and he would see what he could do. Well, he was able to fix it, and everything turned out OK. I think he only charged us $50, which wasn't too bad.

After that, we started walking and as we turned a corner, here sat an old fire engine with people sitting on it, and this guy standing there said, "Would you like to take a ride?" So, we got on, and we went all over, across the Golden Gate Bridge and other places. We had rented a car, and also a cabin in Yosemite National Park, so we headed there. As we entered the park, we came upon this beautiful waterfall; we stopped and took some pictures. Further on, we drove through this huge redwood tree, that you have seen pictures of. When we got to our so-called cabin, it wasn't what we expected — it was a big house. As we started looking over the house, Marlene's phone rang, and as she answered, she started crying, so we knew something was wrong at home. After she hung up, she told us that her Dad had passed away. So, right then, we all decided to return home. Denny said to us that we could stay, but we said we're a team, so we came home, also.

Along with the cruise to Alaska, we went on two others with Denny and Marlene, one to the Caribbean and one to the Hawaiian Islands. The one to the Caribbean was in 1987, and with us, that time, was Pat Winngit, who now is Pat Edwards, and Sandy Scheffel. We stopped at several islands, but I can't remember which ones. I do remember one though, which was Barbados. Denny rented a car, which was very small, and we all barely got in. The roads there are very narrow; as we were driving along, we looked up and saw this rather large truck coming at us, along with a lady walking along the other side of us. I thought, for sure, we were going to hit one or the other, but with luck, we didn't.

I don't remember what year it was that we went to Hawaii, but when we got there, Marilyn made a phone a call to a lady that she had worked with living in Dayton, who had married a guy that was a Hawaiian who had gone to Dayton U. After he graduated, they moved back to his home. The first thing she said to Marilyn, was we were there at the wrong time, because it was going to rain most of the time that we going to be there. We got lucky, since it rained some, but not all the time. The best weather we had, was when we went to a place called Fanny Island; you see, back then, a ship from another country had to go somewhere that wasn't the States, before it could go anywhere in the States, if that makes any sense. During those two days, the weather was great, after that we had some rain, and the ocean was rather rough. At any of the different islands that we visited, we had to take a tender to shore, because there weren't any docks big enough for a ship our size. The four of us went ashore at Pearl Harbor, and visited the Memorial. To our surprise, we saw a lot of Japanese people also visiting the Memorial. Like I said, before, about the seas being rough, we decided to go over that night to a Hawaiian Dinner, which is called a Luau. So, we went top side to board a tender, but when we got there, we saw the tender bouncing up and down pretty much and people coming back off all wet, and one lady was making the sign of the cross on her chest. Marilyn looked at me ,and said that she was not going over to the mainland on the tender, so she and I went to dinner instead. Marlene and Denny went over to the Luau, so after dinner, we went to see the show. While we were watching it, we saw Marlene and Denny come in but they had different clothes on. After the show, we found them and asked them, how come you have different clothes on? They said, on the way back to the ship, a big wave hit the tender and almost drowned them!

We went to Phoenix, AZ, twice, once with Denny and Marlene, and once by ourselves. We went with Denny and Marlene first, and we flew into Phoenix, and rented a van, and then stayed that night in a motel. The next day, we drove to Sedona, and I believe we stayed there at least two days, at a Bed and Breakfast. The owners were real nice; every morning at breakfast, they asked us what we were going to do. I told them that Denny and I wanted to play a round of golf, and that the women wanted to look the town over. So, they took us to the golf course, where we got some golf clubs and met another couple to play with. As we were playing, Denny hit a ball in the water, so Denny takes his shoes off, gets in the water, but one of the couples yells "That's recycled water," and to get out of it. The girls came back to pick us up and we went back to where we were staying, and had dinner. After dinner, we sat around talking, until it was time to go to bed. The morning after, we went to a place where they had horses to ride. We heard that there were a lot of places that you couldn't see, unless you rode a horse. At first, Marilyn said she didn't want to ride a horse, but we told her that we were a team, and that she had to go with us. We did get to see a lot; the earth was a reddish color and the scenery was the same as you see in all the western movies.

The next morning, we drove to Flagstaff, and since it took a while to get there, we stopped to eat lunch. While we were eating, someone asked us where we were going, so we told them we were going to the Grand

Canyon, so guess what the person said to us? "Oh, that's just a big hole in the ground." Can you believe that? We stayed in one of the Lodges at the Canyon that night. The next morning, we walked over to the trail, going down into the Canyon, and started down. We were told that going down is not too bad, but coming back it gets tougher, so they told us to take a lot of water and a snack. Going down, we came to a lady coming up, and she looked beat. There was a rest area about half way down, so we decided to stop, turn around and go back up. On our way back up, we found out quick what they meant about it being tough, since we had to stop several times, and guess what? — that lady we passed going down, we passed again going up.

I don't remember what the date was, but it was some time in 1999, that I get this phone call from the Cincy Enquirer, telling me that they got our number out of the phone book by throwing a dart at it. I said, "Come on, you are kidding me," but he said, "Here is my phone number, call me back." Sure enough, when I called, I got the Enquirer, and they put me through to this person. He told me that they were doing this every Friday, to find out if there's anything interesting. I told him about my time in the service and some other things, but he said nothing like that was interesting. So, I told him my wife and I have belonged to a group since 1968, when we got married, and we get together the last Saturday of every month and every New Year's Day. The great thing about our group is everybody gets along with each other, and when someone needs help with something, we all pitch in and help, like in 1990, when I needed a new roof put on my house. I told him that we were going to meet this New Year's, at Dave's house, in Miamisburg. So, the paper sent a reporter and a camera man to his house, and took our picture, and it was put the paper that next Friday, and that picture is hanging in our family room today. Guess what happened the next day, which was Saturday? I went to the hardware store and there was another man there, and he says to me, "Hey, I saw your picture in the paper this morning." How about that?

Marilyn retired in 1999 or 2000, I can't remember, after which, we started going down to Florida with Ron and Jo from Feb. to March. Along with us, there were four other couples from church that went down also. We all went to Destin, which is on the Gulf Coast. Some went down before us, and came back after us. The first year we went down, we met another couple that was already there. Marilyn worked with the wife at Monsanto; they were Rosalie and Charlie Ostermeier. The four of us decided to go over to Pensacola, where they have an Air Museum, like the one in Dayton. There's a man that's a guide there that Rosalie and Marilyn worked with, at Monsanto. He was a guide on a bus, so we waited until he pulled up in front of the building, and got off; at first he didn't recognize either of the women, then all at once, he said, "I know you, but you should not be here." We had a nice visit with him.

I believe we went down there five years; most of the guys played golf. We all had apartments, so we could visit each other, and we played cards and other games. In the evenings, we would all go to dinner together, and on Sundays, we went to church together. You know how it is, when you get a lot of friends together like that — you can have a lot of fun, which we did. The weather down there wasn't too bad, and it was a lot better than at home. Going down, we usually took two days, but coming home, I drove straight back, most of the time. The first time we went down, we decided to go east to visit with Pat and Eddie Edwards, near Melbourne, Florida; it took us most of the day, because it was 500 miles away, and we stayed there a couple days, then started home.

As we started to leave, it started to rain and it rained all the way home, even though we made a couple more stops. One, was in Atlanta to visit with a couple; Marilyn worked with the lady, but I forget her name. Here it is, raining, and it's dark, and I don't know where I'm going, but we finally found where we had to turn off and got there about an hour later. We stayed overnight, got up the next morning, and it's still raining, and left. As we approached the mountains of Tennessee, it started snowing, and right away, Marilyn said, "Ken, take it slow," so I did. I got in the right-hand lane and stayed there all the way over the mountains. We had one more stop to make before we got home, and that was at Barb and Bill's house, in Lexington, Kentucky. We got there before dark. Barb knew we were coming, so she had supper ready. We stayed overnight, and came home the next morning.

I think in the Fall of 2002, Marilyn and I, with Jo and Ron, drove up to Pennsylvania, to the Civil War Battle Field of Gettysburg, and when we got there, we were able to get a DVD that we could play in our car, that told us where to go next. Gettysburg is a huge battleground, and it would take a long time to walk it, that's why you had to drive through it. That's where I found out that I had to get my left knee worked on, because when we had to walk to some of the sites, I had a hard time doing it. From there, we drove up Hershey, Penn. and went through the Chocolate Factory. We saw how they made the different candy. Then, we got on a bus and they handed us a bunch of different candy bars; the driver told us when each bar was made. The whole trip was interesting.

The year 2003, I had my left knee replaced. I forget who told me, but the doctor that did it, was Dr. Prius, he was supposed to be the best. The first time I saw him, I liked him because he was so down to earth, so to speak. After the operation, my blood sugar count went sky high, and that's when I found out that I was diabetic. I was in the hospital for three days, had some physical therapy, came home, and had this lady, who was a physical therapist, came to the house for four weeks and did the therapy with me. The first day she came and checked how far I could bend my knee, which wasn't too far, she said you might have to go back to the doctor and they would put me under and work the knee real hard. She said, "You don't want that, so keep working hard with the therapy," which I did. At that time, the knee would only go to 80 degrees, but they wanted it to go to 90 plus. So, I really worked hard at it, and on the last day of the rehab, she came in and said, "Show me what you got." So, I went into the living room and sat down in a chair, and pushed my leg back as far as it would go, and she checked the angle of the leg, and it was back more than 90 degrees. She then said, "Do it three times," which I did, and she said, "You're done," and that was it.

Like I said, before, we took a lot of trips with Marlene and Denny, Jo and Ron. We went to D.C. with Ron and Jo, to see the World War II and also the Korean Memorials. Before we got there, we stopped overnight and spent the night at a motel, and saw a sign, stating that for this amount of money, they would drive you to D.C. and take you where you wanted to go. Give you time to see what you wanted to see, then pick you up and take you to the next place. The person was a woman, and we were glad that we went with her, because the traffic was terrible, but we found out real quick what she was going to do. You see, going into D.C., there's a left lane that's open for cars that have four or more people in them, so we just bused by all the other cars. After we visited some of the memorials, it was almost noon time; our driver said she knew a little place that she always went for lunch. When we got there and were eating, we looked up to see what was on the T.V. We saw a lot of cop cars running towards the Capitol Building. While we were watching, the announcer said that the Capitol had been closed, because someone came in with a costume on, and carrying a toy gun. It was right around Halloween time, and we found out that the person that did this worked in the Capitol.

A couple times, we went to Gatlinburg, with Denny and Marlene, once with another couple, and another time with the boys. As you all know, I'm well known for my apple cake and I took one with us. So, the couple that went with us, was the first time they had a chance to eat it. Their names are Scott and Lauria Gruner; anyway getting back to the cake, every time you looked, here's Scott getting into it.

On Feb. 22, 2007, we took another trip; we flew from Cincy to Phoenix, AZ. We were going to visit Georgia & Ron Woebkenberg, in Sun City, AZ. They have a home here, in Blue Ash. Their boys and ours went to school together and also played soccer on the same teams that Ron and I coached together. We visited with them for four days, and from their home, the four of us drove to the Grand Canyon Railway Hotel at Williams, AZ. We stayed overnight, and boarded the Grand Canyon Railway, for a trip to the Grand Canyon. We returned to Williams around 6:00 pm, and then traveled about 2 hours to our hotel, on the way to Las Vegas. We stayed overnight, and the next day, drove to Harrah's Hotel in Las Vegas. We stayed there two days, playing the slots, and checking out all the huge hotels, where the casinos were. From there, we drove to the Hoover Dam, which is a sight to see! Construction of Hoover Dam began in 1931, the year I was born, how about that? The last concrete was poured in 1935, and even with the remote location and some of the harshest working conditions, it was completed two years ahead of schedule, and well under budget. It was named the number five construction achievement of the 20th century. It can hold 9.2 trillion gallons of water. Hoover Dam is named for Herbert Hoover, the 31st President of the United States; it was also called Boulder Dam, and the name, Hoover, was made permanent in 1947. From there, we went back to their house and visited a couple more days and flew back home.

That same year, Todd was working for a place that belonged to a company from Italy, and he went over to Italy, because of his job, for three months. Before he went over, a fellow with his family came over here. Their name is Pascale — Pietro, Maria, and daughter, Ginevra. It was getting close to Easter, at the time, and as you know, we always had Easter with the family, here. Anyway, Todd asked us if it would be OK if he could invite them to come, and of course, we said yes. Then, later that year, Todd with his family, went back over to Italy and stayed for four months. More about them later.

Pietro stayed a couple of months, and went back home. Then, in 2008, he brought his wife and daughter over here to live. I think they rented a house in Madeira, and Ginevra, their daughter, ended up being in the same grade in school with Sam. March of 2007, I was having a lot of pain in my shoulders, so I went to see an orthopedic doctor. Dr. Thomas was his name, and I asked him if he was a shoulder doctor, and he said he was, so I asked him if he was any good. He just laughed and said, "I think so." He took some X-rays and asked me which one hurt the most and I told him that my left did. He said that my right one looked the worst, but he will do the left first. I was in the hospital three days, came home, had some rehab, and then back to the building where my doctor was and had more rehab. Then, in 2008, I had the right shoulder done, and went through the same process.

Sometime, during the year of 2010, Marilyn was having trouble with one of her feet, and she went to a foot doctor and got something to take. She went back the next week, and she did this for several weeks, but it didn't help. I told her that I wasn't going back to him, because all he was doing was taking her money. I think about that time she was supposed to see Dr. Lohr, to check how everything was with the cancer that she had in '98. As soon as the doctor walked in, she looked at Marilyn, and said "Oh Marilyn, you are in trouble." So, she set up an appointment for her to get an X-ray taken. Jo Ann and I went with her when she got it, and went back with the person that was about to read the results. All he said was that he could see a large mass in the liver, but he couldn't tell us what it was because, he didn't know.

We went to see Dr. Lohr at Beth. Hospital, and she said she wanted to go a little further, and take an MRI of that area. After that, we went back to Dr. Lohr's office, on the western part of town, and that's when we got the bad news. She told us that Marilyn had a 70 per cent Melanoma of the liver. Then, the doctor asked if there was anything else she having trouble with, and I said, "She's having trouble walking." Doc. Lohr said, "I'll be right back." and when she came back, she told us to take her right now, to Good Sam Hospital, to find out what was going on with her back. They will be waiting for you, and when we got there, they took her right away to X-ray and that's when we found out that she had cancer of the spine. That was in Sept 2011, and I think they gave her some radiation treatments, while she was there. On that following Sunday, Scott, Todd and I went to see her, and they told us that she had to be out of the hospital by Monday, so we walked outside of the room to talk things over, and I came up with the idea that we could put her in hospice, until I could fix up the living room, with a hospital bed, so she could look out the front window, and not be in a dark room. She heard us talking and said, "You mean that I only have two weeks to live?" and we told her no, that we needed time to get everything ready at home, so we can get you there. She talked to everyone while at the hospital, but as soon as we got her to hospice, she quit. As you all know, she didn't last two weeks, she only lasted six more days, and she left us, to be with our Lord, up in Heaven. She passed away Oct. 1, 2011.

When Ron died, Jo had him cremated and had a memorial service for him at church. Marilyn and I liked that, so we thought that was good idea, so we said to each other, "Let's do the same thing," so that's what we did for her. I had her cremated and her remains put in a jar that's used for that purpose, and it sits in the bay window in the family room, so when I go, the kids will put both of us in the same grave.

The night, before the memorial, everyone was at the house, getting pictures ready for the service the next day, even Pietro's family was here. I happened to look up once, and guess what I saw, here's Pietro putting pictures in one of the frames, I said to him, "Pietro, as of right now, you are my fifth son, and Maria you are my fifth daughter-in-law, and Ginevra, you are my new granddaughter," and she looked up at me and said OK.

In fact, both sides of the family welcomed them as part of our family. They fit in, just like a pair of gloves. Just to show you how: a couple years ago, they bought this big house with a swimming pool, and Scott's and Todd's families and I went there the summer of 2013. We got to talking about who was going to have Thanksgiving that year, since Jo didn't have her house anymore. Guess what? Maria said, "I'll do it," and she did a great job.

The year 2012, while working at the golf course, I this funny feeling in my chest, and said to myself, I better get this checked out. I went to my family doctor and he sent me downstairs to the ER. The doctor checked me over, and said, "I don't think it's your heart, but I want you to stay here over night." I told him, "No way, because my grandson has a ball game tomorrow and I'm not going to miss it." They called me the next Monday, and told me that I'm to see a cardiologist next, and they are going to run some tests. So, the next day, I went for the tests and the first one I did was on the treadmill. The lady that gave me the test said that everything went well and everything is OK. I forget what they did next, but they did something to see if I had any blockage of my valves and arteries, and they turned out being clear. But I still had that same feeling in my chest, so I went to see Dr. Lohr, and she had me get an X-ray of my chest. It showed that I had a problem with my gallbladder. I had to go to Good Sam Hospital for that, and I ended up staying an extra night because the doctor said that were so many stones in there, that they wanted to make sure that they removed all of them.

March 2013, I had my right knee replaced, but instead of having my rehab at home, I went to a place called Chesterwood Village on Tylersville Road. It was a really nice place, and the first time I went to rehab, this gal said to me, "I'm going to hurt you," and I said to her, "You can't hurt this old Marine!" She tried, but she failed. I was there four days, got my knee back to where it had to be and went back home.

The winter of 2014, was a bad year for me and my next door neighbor, Art Henderson. In January, we had a lot of snow and ice and along with it, it was so cold. One day, I'm out there with my snow blower, and slipped on the ice and could not get up. Well, Art and Greg from up the street came down and helped get me up. I went and got my back checked and found out that I had arthritis in my back, so the doctor had me get some rehab for my back. I'm still doing the rehab today. Then, one morning, as I was fixing my breakfast, my right hip gave out on me, so I went back to the doc, and he said that I had arthritis in my hips. So, then, I started using a walker in the house or if I went anywhere. Then, in March, when I went to work at the golf course, I asked my boss if it was OK if I used the walker and he said yes, so I used it a couple weeks. Then, I started using a cane. Then, one day, during that spring, the kids all came to the house and cleaned out my flower garden in the front of the house. While they were here, they said to me, Dad we want you to stay in your house as long as you're able, and to work at the golf course as long as you can, but we're going to get you some help. I had a guy already coming to cut my grass every week. At that time, Karin and Ryan would come and eat lunch with me once in awhile, and she said I have this cleaning company coming today, to talk to us. Their name was Visiting Angels; the man told us it would cost me $35 an hour, and someone would come and clean the house. He also sold me a medical alert for $300, with no monthly fees. Well, the first time this lady came, she worked for about an hour, then came into the room, where I was reading a book and sat down. I said to her, "Do you do windows?" and she said, "No, I only do light work." Then, I asked her, "Are you done working?" and she said "Yes, and I'm supposed to sit and talk to you." So, I told her that she could leave and not to come back. I called Karin, and told her, I'm paying $35 dollars an hour for someone to come and talk to me! With this, she said she had someone else that she called, that told her that the first three times were free, because of me being a veteran. She called them, and they told her that someone would be here the next Monday.

That day, I was sitting in living room, when I heard a car door close and looked out the window and saw these two women coming up the walk with big smiles on their faces, I said to myself, this is going to be good. Like I said before, the first three times were free, and that first time, they were here almost eight hours. They come once a mouth, and it costs $149.47, no matter how long they are here.

A couple weeks later, as I pulled in my driveway, I saw them helping Art get out of his car. They told me that the doctor said they think that he has Parkinson's disease. Later, I found out that he had, and I don't how to spell it, but here goes, Alzheimer's disease. I don't know a lot about it, but I thought that you had it for a while, before it took you. Not with him. At first, he couldn't walk, and it got so bad, they had to put him in a nursing home. While there, he kept getting worse, and it finally took him. He was only 72, and he was my neighbor for 39 years.

Dec. of this year, 2014, I had cataracts taken off my eyes, and ended up with 20/20 vision, and the only time I need glasses, is when I read anything. Not bad for an old man of 83.

• • •

Since it's been a while since I started this thing, let me update you on my family. The date is Feb. 11, 2015.

Steve, my first, was born Aug. 23, 1953, wife Linda, Mar. 29, 1954, daughter Erin, Sept. 27, 1974, son-in-law Chris, Apr. 10, 1974, grandsons, Casey Dec.3, 2001, Brady Nov. 27, 2003, Riley Feb.14, 2005; son, Josh, Feb.10, 1976, daughter-in-law, Marcie, April 22 1976. 115

Doug, my second born, Dec.4, 1956, wife Terry April 17, 1962, son Ben Oct 5, 1992, daughters, Kate Aug. 24, 1995, and Andrea, March 18, 1999.

Scott, my third born, Aug.17 1969, wife Greta, April 25, 1975, daughter, Emily Jan.14, 2001, son Sam, July 8 2003.

Todd, my fourth born, July 6, 1972, wife Karin, June 10, 1972, sons Colin, Aug. 21, 2004, Ryan, June 13, 2006.

This year, I'll start my 19th year at the golf course. Hopefully, more years after that, God willing.

Your Author,

*Ken Eppert*

P.S. I had a good time doing this, and I think everyone should do the same to let the next of kin that come after you are gone, know how things were, during the time you were on earth. I know that it's taken me a long time doing this, and I've jumped around quite a lot, but while doing this, I kept remembering a lot of different things that have happened to me.

Honor Flight in Washington, DC

# PHOTO ALBUM

Myself and Shirley on our wedding day

Cutting the Cake

Myself, Shirley and Vern

Myself Shirley with sons Steve and Doug

# Photo Album

Myself and Shirley deep sea fishing

George and Dorothy Lowenstein (Shirley's sister who with her husband George raised her after their mother's death at 13). Ironically after Shirley's death they served to be an integral part in helping me raise Steve and Doug, ages 13 and 10.

My Mother and Stepfather

My Father, Grandfather, myself, and Steve in my lap

My sister, Linda, and her husband Bob

Doug, Bob, Linda, Stepmother, Steve and my Father, Edgar

My brother, Marion

Marion's son Jay

Marilyn and I on our wedding day

Cruising

Photo Album

# Family

Todd, Scott, Pops, Doug and Steve

Scott, Todd, Pops, Marilyn, Steve, Linda, Doug

Doug, Scott, Dorothy, Marilyn, Pop's and Todd

Pops and the four boys at Wrigley

Steve, Doug, Pops, Todd and Scott

# My Four Sons and Their Families
# Also my fifth, Italian Son

Erin, Josh, Linda and Steve

Terry, Ben, Katie, Andrea and Doug

Greta, Sam, Scott and Emily

Karin, Ryan, Colin and Todd

Pietro, Ginevra and Maria

## American Heroes Getting Their Day in the Sun

Always Sharing

Back among Family where happiness is

Scott's Band TWIG. Mike, Dave, Mark and Scott. Pops never misses a show.

Many Birthday Parties

Todd and Pietro "Our Pops' proclaimed fifth son"

Todd, Pops and Doug

## My Entire Immediate Family

Back: Ben, Doug, Terry, Katie, Linda, Steve, Josh, Marci, Scott, Greta and Chris Tucker (Erin's husband)

Middle Back: Andrea, Colin, Ryan, Sam, Emily

Middle Front: Todd, Brady, Pops, Marilyn, Erin

Floor and Laps: Karin, Riley, Casey

Makes everyone around him smile even when he is not

All this writing; I need a NAP!!!

www.ingramcontent.com/pod-product-compliance
Lightning Source LLC
Chambersburg PA
CBHW070459100426
42743CB00010B/1686